THE HARVEST O

The Church of El Salvador
Ten Years After Romero

DANIEL SANTIAGO

PAULIST PRESS
New York/Mahwah

Library of Congress Cataloging-in-Publication Data

Santiago, Daniel.
    The harvest of justice: the church of El Salvador ten years after Romero/Daniel Santiago.
      p. cm.
    Includes bibliographical references.
    ISBN 0-8091-3446-2 (pbk.)
    1. Catholic Church—El Salvador—History—20th century. 2. El Salvador—History—1979- 3. El Salvador—Church history. 4. Christianity and justice—Catholic Church. 5. Catholic Church—Doctrines. I. Title.
BX1446.2.S26   1993
282'.7284'09049—dc20
                                  93-31247
                                      CIP

Published by Paulist Press
997 Macarthur Boulevard
Mahwah, New Jersey 07430

Printed and bound in the United States of America

CONTENTS

Dedicated to Archbishop Arturo Rivera Damas,
Monsignor Ricardo Urioste and
Father Fabian Amaya-Torres.

"My prayer is that your love may more and more abound, both in understanding and wealth of experience, so that with a clear conscience and blameless conduct you may learn to value the things that really matter, to the very day of Christ. It is my wish that you may be found rich in the harvest of justice which Jesus Christ has ripened in you, to the glory and praise of God."

Philippians 1:9-11

INTRODUCTION

Maria Luisa Lopez' home sits on the base of the volcano of San Vicente in the country of El Salvador. The small compound surrounding her house is protected by a fence made of bamboo, pieces of discarded wood and scraps of metal. The gate is a metal box spring, tied to a post with baling wire.

Maria Luisa's kitchen is a bamboo and thatch lean-to located in the center of this compound. She spends most of her days there, either preparing meals for her grandchildren or weaving baskets for sale in San Salvador's central market. Her granddaughters have learned to weave baskets and, now that the oldest is thirteen, Maria Luisa has turned over responsibility for market days to the girls. Her two grandsons work in the fields with their uncles, planting and harvesting corn and beans from May until October, and picking coffee in November and December. There is no work for the rest of the year.

"These are Roberto's children," Maria Luisa told me at the time of my first visit. "They were not born here on San Vicente, but in the capital—in San Salvador. The oldest girl, Estela, has completed fourth grade and we are quite proud of her. Even little Delmi completed one year of schooling before they came back to live with me.

"They are like my Roberto. Full of questions and always wanting to know why we do things this way and not that. And I suppose Roberto was like me and that is why they killed him."

Roberto Lopez was Maria Luisa's oldest son. He left rural San Vicente in 1974 to work in a factory in San Salvador. There, Roberto met a young woman, Virgilia Sanchez. Roberto and Virgilia eventually married and had five children. Both became active in a labor union as well as in a small Christian community that met in the Mejicanos section of San Salvador. They survived the great persecution directed against the base communities in the early 1980s and eventually went to work as community organizers. Virgilia was killed in October 1986

1

during an earthquake that destroyed much of the capital. The following May Roberto was captured by the treasury police.

"They took my boy to the treasury police headquarters and kept him for three weeks. They did awful things to him. They starved him and then fed him rotten food. They covered his head with a cement bag filled with lime and beat him with a bamboo rod. As he gasped, he breathed in the lime, burning his lungs and slowly turning them to stone. When he was finally released, he had few marks on his body but inside he was dying.

"Roberto came home to live with me and to die with me. At night I'd hold him in my arms and wipe his lips as he coughed up blood. He couldn't eat. Drinking water caused him terrible pain. He could not talk much during those last days, but when he did, my boy told me about his work with the Christian base communities. He told me about the Bible and how God favored the poor. He told me about Monseñor Romero and about the struggle for justice.

"I never heard these things from the bishop of San Vicente or from any of his priests. But coming with the last gasps of my son's life, I believed. And in the few years since he has died, I've become active in the struggle for liberation. I have joined a Christian base community and studied the Bible. I've found truths there that I never heard in church. I have also found the strength to raise my son's children as he wished them to be raised."

Maria Luisa is still a basket maker. She has also become a "delegate of the word." Together with a friend and her oldest granddaughter, Maria Luisa visits small communities in San Vicente, leading the people in discussions about the Bible. These discussions include analysis of the Salvadoran reality. For this reason her work is dangerous. "But others take greater risks than I do," Maria Luisa told me. "You should talk with them. Listen to their stories. See the work of the communities. Then decide what you must do."

This book is comprised of stories of the Salvadoran people and their interpretation of the conflict that has ripped apart their country in the years since the death of Archbishop Oscar Romero. These chapters reflect a style born out of the conditions under which they were written. They are short and lack much in the way of scholarly references. This is because they were written in locales frequently searched by military patrols, thus preventing the use of library and files. They reflect an interest in what was taking place at the time they were written: between 1990 and 1992 amidst brutal military recruitment, increased violence directed against poor communities, torture and assassination. They reflect the excitement generated by the continuing efforts of poor communities to organize and Archbishop Rivera Damas' decision to submit Oscar Romero's "cause" to the Vatican for beatification. They exhibit the anticipation and trepidation of the poor as the Salvadoran resistance, the FMLN, negotiated a cease-fire with the government of El Salvador.

Details from these testimonies have been changed to protect the identity of the communities and individuals who speak here. The security of these men and women is more important than providing a historical record of particular dates, persons and communities engaged in the struggle for liberation. More precise documentation and evidence for the tragedy of El Salvador is readily available, however, from the Catholic Church's human rights office, Tutela Legal, Amnesty International, America's Watch, the Washington Office on Latin America (WOLA) and other groups monitoring the human rights situation and the implementation of the peace accords.

I write this book for North Americans who are deeply troubled by what has happened in Central America and by the government of the United States' complicity in these events.

I write to confront my readers with the appalling evil of Salvadoran militarization, a social force that remains in El Salvador even though the Salvadoran resistance, the FMLN, and the government of El Salvador have negotiated a cease fire. The first section to this book is called "A Kingdom Without Justice." A decade after the death of Oscar Romero and after ten years of United States military aid, El Salvador has become a kingdom without justice—a large band of robbers.

United States military aid has contributed to the militarization of all sectors of Salvadoran society. For example, an association of retired and active military officers is now the largest real estate developer in El Salvador. Military officers control the most important agencies of the government. The military exerts control over the judicial system. Military values—conformity, acquiescence, unquestioning obedience to "legitimate authority"—exert a great influence on popular culture. The military promotes these values through its manipulation of the press, television, the arts, and public education. They regard as subversive: non-conformity, creativity and independent community initiatives. In El Salvador, the consequences for subversion are high. The deaths have mounted in the years since the assassination of

Archbishop Oscar Arnulfo Romero. North Americans need to confront their culpability in this travesty of justice.

I write to show how, in the midst of this evil, the people of El Salvador have said yes to life and have organized themselves to resist death. The second section of this book is called "Faithful Endurance." Despite the terrible power of the military within their society, valiant men and women have remained faithful to the gospel and have endured in their struggle for peace with justice in El Salvador. They have done so with creativity and tenacity. Some joined the armed resistance, the FMLN. Many others became active in popular organizations and base communities. Others agitate for greater participation by the poor in El Salvador's social and economic life.

It is true, these efforts pale in their overall impact. The number of people who participate in Christian base communities represents a small percentage of the overall church-going population. The hundreds of thousands who receive medical assistance through church-sponsored clinics constitute a small portion of the millions who lack adequate medical care. The small cooperatives—bakeries, seamstress shops, craft workshops, carpentry shops, brick foundries and metal forges—that are sponsored by the popular organizations, unions and churches, make a minuscule contribution to El Salvador's gross national product. The thousands of refugees and displaced persons who have formed cooperative communities are a fragment of the many who still live in exile or are homeless. But these meager efforts stand out as bold alternatives to the armed forces' vision of a homogeneous military state where everyone knows one's place, dutifully obeys authority and waits upon the powerful to decide his or her destiny.

I write to share the faith of a people who, through their suffering and sacrifice, have planted the seeds of a new kingdom of peace with justice in the soil of El Salvador. The third section of this book is called "*Kairos* El Salvador." It describes how the Salvadoran people's witness to the struggle for justice has been expressed in traditional and new forms of faith-sharing. Salvadoran base communities meet under conditions not unlike those of the primitive Christian communities. Like those early Christians, members of these communities have created kerygmatic texts that testify to a faith formed in the crucible of suffering. These texts and the witness of the communities challenge all who profess belief in the gospel of Jesus Christ.

Salvadorans speak of the years since Romero's death as a time of *kairos*, God's special time. When Salvadoran communities receive visitors, or when representatives of the communities visit the United

States, they do so principally to share their *kairos* faith. For them, this sharing is more important than fund-raising and political lobbying. It is essential to the life of the church; it constitutes its catholicity. It is equally important for North Americans to listen to these modern-day apostles.

I write to raise a suspicion. The guerrillas of the FMLN and the government of El Salvador signed a peace agreement on January 16, 1992. What has changed in El Salvador as a result of this peace accord? Little, except that the conditions for negotiating necessary social changes are now present. The fourth section of this book is called "Wanting Peace, Working for Justice." It was written immediately before, during and in the six months after the signing of the peace accord. These final five essays reflect the skepticism, initial elation, disillusionment and reassessment of the meaning of peace experienced by many Salvadorans in the first six months of 1992.

El Salvador certainly needs a pastoral of hope to accompany its pastoral of liberation. And in this light, the peace accords should be applauded and both sides encouraged to follow them. But hoping for peace in El Salvador should not become a veil laid over the suffering of that tortured people. As the testimonies presented in this book make clear, the armed forces of El Salvador are an institution apart from the people and apart from the government that pretends to represent the people. While constitutionally bound to follow the peace accords, the Salvadoran military have never subjected themselves to civilian control. The pervasive evil of the armed forces of El Salvador remains fueled with American aid. The armed forces also remain locked in deadly combat with the church of El Salvador.

Will the church of El Salvador finally be able to reap the harvest of justice it deserves? After so much death by sword, so many captured, tortured and disappeared, after sowing the ground for so many years with the blood of martyrs, will poor communities finally be able to organize without fear? Will catechists be able to teach and bishops preach without the threat of death? Will unions be able to meet, to demand higher wages and to strike? The challenge before the Salvadoran people is to faithfully endure. The challenge before the church of North America is to continue to be vigilant, to watch, to listen and, when appropriate, to act.

Part One:
A KINGDOM WITHOUT JUSTICE

"What are kingdoms without justice, but large bands of robbers?"

St. Augustine

The chapters in "Part One: A Kingdom Without Justice" show the effects of militarization on the people of El Salvador. There are other sources, broader in scope and more comprehensive, that describe the command structure and organization of El Salvador's armed forces. While it is important to understand such structures, these chapters assume another perspective on militarization—that of the subjective experience of poor communities who lived through twelve years of war and regard the de-militarization of their society as a national priority.

The military and security forces of El Salvador act independently of the elected government. They have killed leftist political leaders with impunity and denied progressive elected officials access to office. The military's character and self-identity are significant obstacles to peace in El Salvador. The armed forces hold themselves accountable to their own military tradition, not to a constitution. Military ideals and the needs of military men provide the armed forces with their code of conduct. While these ideals, needs and codes are spurned by the vast majority of enlisted men, they are carefully cultivated by the fraternity of officers and by the military academies. The phrase "reform of the Salvadoran military" expresses an understatement when one considers the deep-seated evil permeating the Salvadoran armed forces and the changes that are necessary before that institution will be inclined to serve democracy in El Salvador.

7

During the war, this evil was clearly felt in small, rural communities and city barrios whenever the military was present. It was seen in a mother's terror when she went to the police station to reclaim the tortured body of a daughter or son. Sometimes, the simple act of reclaiming the body of a death squad victim was interpreted by the military as support for the Salvadoran resistance, and families and whole communities were punished as a result.

Young people felt the effects of militarization at the beginning and end of every month. These were recruitment days when truckloads of national guardsmen or civilian defense forces scoured bus stops, schools, soccer fields and other haunts for young men.

Removing corrupt officers and those responsible for heinous crimes is an important step in El Salvador's national reconciliation. But much more is needed. Military recruits are still victimized by the Salvadoran armed forces. The armed forces' lack of public accountability isolates recruits from the society at large. Soldiers and their families are regarded with suspicion in their communities. Militarization thrives on such fear and mistrust, both of which gnaw at the fabric of community.

If reconciliation is to come to El Salvador, the events described in the following chapters must be made public. What is more, great efforts must be made to radically transform the institutions responsible for committing these crimes. The struggle for justice is now a struggle to battle the military's ongoing effort to obfuscate the historical record. The testimonies of the suffering poor, their dreams for peace and commitment to struggle even while being terrorized by the military—these signs of the times proclaim that faith is stronger than violence.

The suffering of the poor at the hands of the military leads to a straightforward mandate for North Americans. Members of communities that have been brutally victimized over the past ten years express this mandate with stark simplicity. "Tell your people to send no more weapons of war, no more bombs and no more airplanes. We've had enough now." It is all the more important to heed this plea given the peace agreement of January 16, 1992.

THE AESTHETICS OF TERROR
The Hermeneutics of Death

I have heard Toñita tell her story a dozen times. She recounted the horror for each delegation of North Americans who visited the refugee camp on the outskirts of San Salvador. With so many tellings Toñita's testimony acquired a repetitive quality. When translated and transcribed it is somewhat unbelievable. What convinces, however, is not the story itself, but Toñita's visceral reaction to each telling. Her tears are not the stage tears of an actress; the lines of pain that cross her wrinkled face have not been enhanced with make-up. I have stayed with Toñita once the visitors had left the camp. I have held her as she vomited the nausea that comes with each retelling and wiped her tears on my shirt. Toñita's story is quite believable, and that is the problem.

Toñita is a peasant from Santa Lucia, a rural village near the volcano of San Vicente in the country of El Salvador. On June 20, 1987, at eleven in the morning, Toñita left her one-room home to carry lunch to her husband, Chepe, and two teenage sons who were cutting firewood on the volcano. She left her three smallest children—an eighteen month old daughter, a three year old son and a five year old daughter—in the care of her sister and mother.

It took Toñita an hour to find Chepe and the boys. She sat with them while they ate. She joked with her sons about their soccer team's string of losses during the past season. Toñita lingered after Chepe and the boys had finished eating. She washed the plates, cups and plastic lunch bucket in a nearby stream. When she was ready to depart, Chepe tied a load of wood onto Toñita's back. Toñita picked up her bucket and began the return trip home, feeling slightly guilty for leaving her younger children in the care of others for such a long time.

Toñita and Chepe's house sat on ten acres of farmland on the outskirts of Santa Lucia. Like most Salvadorans, they owned their

9

house but leased the land. Three other families lived near Toñita and Chepe, and the area in front of the four houses was normally filled with chickens, ducks, playing children and gossiping old people. But on this day, as Toñita approached her home, she noticed that something was wrong. The chickens and ducks were there, but there were no children or elders to be seen.

Toñita hurried forward. She dropped her load of firewood and Chepe's lunch bucket as she approached her house. Entering, Toñita was greeted by the grisly spectacle of a feast *macabre*. Seated around a small table in the middle of her house was her mother, sister and three children. The decapitated heads of all five had been placed in front of each torso, their hands arranged on top, as if each body was stroking its own head. This had proven difficult in the case of the youngest daughter. The difficulty had been overcome by nailing the hands onto the head. The hammer had been left on the table. The floor and table were awash with blood. In the very center of the table was a large plastic bowl filled with blood; the air hung heavy with its sweet, cloying smell.

Toñita stood transfixed in the doorway. She did not scream. She did not cry. She simply let out a low moan—one that started in her bowels and accumulated layers of pain and grief as it made its way up through her throat and passed her lips.

Toñita's neighbors had fled when the Salvadoran national guard had begun their killing. The *guardia* had not tried to stop the people from fleeing; indeed, they encouraged it. One neighbor, Doña Laura, returned for Toñita and found her standing in the doorway, moaning and staring at her decapitated mother, sister and children.

Doña Laura took Toñita from the house. The two women joined the thousands of peasants fleeing the terror of war and the uncertainty of life. They wondered, "What other horrors are possible from men who could cut off the head of an eighteen month old baby?" In El Salvador, this is not a flippant question. It is a serious question with grievous consequences.

Toñita did not see Chepe or her two boys after she left Santa Lucia. She worried about them, of course, but eventually learned that they were alive and fighting the *guardia* in the Province of Chalatenango.

This chapter is not about Toñita, her family or the other victims of El Salvador's war. It is about the aesthetics of terror and the hermeneutics of death—how people were killed in El Salvador and how killing was interpreted during the twelve year war and how it is being interpreted now, in its aftermath. Most Americans were numbed by the news that came out of El Salvador during the war— 75,000 victims, the bombing of poor barrios, the disappearance, capture, torture and killing of students and union leaders, the assassination of an archbishop, the massacre of priests and rape of nuns. But the scale of killing in El Salvador was so large it prevented us from appreciating its grim artistry—its aesthetics.

It is easy to understand two armies posed in battle and fighting over the spoils of a country. One can even understand why, in a class war like El Salvador's, the national guard would kill a peasant family. But why this attention to detail? Why such a carefully orchestrated tableau? North Americans read descriptions of these killings with the same kind of morbid fascination that they read of the Nazi death camps. How is such cruelty possible? The mind may strive for clarity, but it is also fascinated by the muddle of the aesthetics of terror.

We need to understand these events, not only because our tax dollars helped to fund them, but because it is our nature to strive to understand. In El Salvador's insurrection there were two distinct styles of killing, one assumed by the guerrillas, the second by the armed forces and death squads. The guerrillas were artists of death and critics of their own style. They admitted when they killed and they interpreted their killing. Ironically, they said that they killed to force an end to the killing. Thus, they killed as many soldiers as possible; they did this as quickly as they could, and wherever they could find them. It was easy for North Americans to understand the guerrillas' style of making war. It was the aesthetic of killing that normally governs American war-making. (Mai Lai was the aberration, not the norm.) The guerrillas wanted to kill Salvadoran soldiers to force the government to undertake the structural changes required to make El Salvador a just society.

While one may disagree with the guerrillas' definition of justice, there is no disputing that the way they made war was consistent with their goals. According to Salvadoran government and independent sources, these guerrillas had six thousand men under arms. These six thousand guerrillas were an effective military force that kept the Salvadoran armed forces at bay for over ten years. The effectiveness of the guerrillas was further underscored by the disparity in the resources available to both sides. For ten years the guerrillas received some international support through Nicaragua, although this source was closed to them with the fall of the Sandinistas. The armed forces, on the other hand, were fueled daily with one and a half million dollars in American aid.

But these figures do not tell the whole story. The Salvadoran armed forces also had a different aesthetic than the guerrillas. They did not just kill; they killed with style.

Return to the massacre of Toñita's family. It takes effort to decapitate old women and small children. It takes imagination to arrange their torsos around the table as if about to share a feast of their own blood. This was only one tableau of many. Other *scenes macabres* were created by the armed forces in their twelve year exhibition of horror and death.

People were not just killed by death squads in El Salvador—they were decapitated and then their heads were placed on pikes and used to dot the landscape.

Men were not just disemboweled by the Salvadoran treasury police; their severed genitalia were stuffed into their mouths.

Salvadoran women were not just raped by the national guard; their wombs were cut from their bodies and used to cover their faces.

It was not enough to kill children; they were dragged over barbed wire until the flesh fell from their bones while parents were forced to watch.

It was not enough to kill priests. The soldiers from the United States-trained Atlacatl battalion who executed six Jesuits in November 1989 blew out the brains of these priests. This was a statement about what the killers think about the valued intellect of the Jesuit. The impulses that gave rise to this aesthetics have not changed with the signing of a peace accord. These are not just killers. These are artisans of terror.

The aesthetics of terror in El Salvador is religious. The armed forces and the ARENA party uphold the religious ideal of *patria*—fatherland. The individual—and individual rights—are subordinated to the interests of the fatherland. One achieves eternal life by identifying with the fatherland and by submitting one's will to that of the leader. ARENA's political rhetoric reflects these religious values. ARENA has announced in the public press that "the interests of the fatherland should be sacred to all citizens." ARENA regards the sacrifice of the individual to the fatherland as a privilege and an honor. ARENA leadership has referred to the death squads as the "Army of National Salvation." ARENA's political motto echoes that of the death squads; it claims to be the "Party of National Salvation."

Any ominous similarity to national socialist (Nazi) idealization of race and national culture is no coincidence. Roberto D'Aubuisson was the "leader-for-life" of ARENA. He died of throat cancer in 1992, shortly after the peace accords were signed. During his lifetime, D'Aubuisson publicly extolled Adolf Hitler and the holocaust. D'Aubuisson was a racist, but racism alone does not account for D'Aubuisson's hatred for the Jews. Rather, he regarded Jews as communists. And communism is opposed to nationalism—the ultimate religious value for ARENA. So why not kill the Jews, and the "dirty little Indians" trying to destroy the *patria*? There are other international organizations that ARENA holds in equal disdain: the Jesuits, the Catholic Church, the United Nations, the International Red Cross...the list is long.

Members of the ARENA party regard party membership as a natural condition. It involves the essence of being—much as being a Nazi was considered an ontological condition. Former United States ambassador to El Salvador Robert White reported in hearings before the House Committee on Foreign Affairs that ARENA is modeled after the Nazis. White further demonstrated how ARENA officials orchestrated the assassination of Archbishop Oscar Romero. He even secured a videotape of D'Aubuisson taking credit for this murder and referring to the archbishop as the "Ayatollah." White did not liken ARENA to national socialism in a metaphorical sense. He showed how ARENA consciously modeled itself on the Nazis.

White's charge has been substantiated by others. It needs to be taken seriously because of its moral consequences. In national socialism the members of the party do not differentiate between the wishes of the leader and their own wishes. Like the S.S. (*Schutzstaffeln*, Protection Squad), ARENA's members take a "blood oath" to the leader. During the Nuremburg war crimes trials the United States insisted that so complete was the Nazis' identification with the party, and so horrible were the Nazi crimes, that membership in the party implied some guilt. One would expect the same to be true of ARENA, but it is not.

ARENA made itself more acceptable to the United States when it nominated Alfredo Cristiani for president. Mr. Cristiani is a graduate of Georgetown University. He is a conservative businessman who has convinced many of his desire to bring peace to El Salvador. He probably finds ARENA's aesthetics of terror repugnant. A liberally-educated fellow like Alfredo Cristiani probably kept his fingers crossed during the blood oath to ARENA's "leader-for-life," Roberto D'Aubuisson. He probably winced when ARENA deputies promised during the 1989 national elections to "get these Jesuits." At night Mr. Cristiani probably complains to his wife about his party's brownshirts. But Mr. Cristiani has not quit ARENA, nor did he ever disassociate himself from the party's "leader for life."

After the November 1989 massacre of Jesuits at the University of Central America, Connecticut's Senator Christopher Dodd pledged continued support to the government of El Salvador because of his personal confidence in Mr. Cristiani. President Bush told the American people that he believed that the murderers of the six Jesuits would be pursued because Mr. Cristiani gave him personal assurances to do so. Senator Dodd would not likely express this kind of confidence in a nice Nazi. President Bush would probably not take a Nazi at his word. But American politicians have made an exception for Mr. Cristiani. He is part of a dirty crowd but he is regarded as respectable.

Dodd was not alone in his displaced loyalty. Many United States senators have announced that the Cristiani government was democratically elected and so deserves American support. But United States senators do not go home at election time, round up their local supporters and wipe out the opposition. This has happened with impunity and regularity in El Salvador.

Various congressional representatives have informed their constituents that "President Cristiani deserves our support" and that he has offered personal guarantees to bring the killers of the six Jesuits to justice. This logic applies in the United States where the citizens drove a president from the White House for lying. But these rules do not hold forth in El Salvador where assassins of archbishops enjoy the support of the government. What many members of the house of representatives have failed to recognize is that Mr. Cristiani cannot improve the situation in El Salvador even if he wanted to do so. Even after the peace accords have been signed, political analysts realize that peace depends on the "goodwill" of the armed forces.

Good will? The Salvadoran armed forces are sadomasochistic. Their killing has sexual overtones. During the war, Salvadorans were not shocked to learn when nuns were raped by the national guard, when teachers and health workers were sexually molested by the treasury police or when peasants were mutilated after they had been killed by the army. It would have been news if these charges were leveled against the asexual guerrillas. But one did not hear these charges made. The guerrillas killed, to be sure, but for them it was an intellectual exercise, not a sexual experience.

The armed forces of El Salvador are to be reduced as a result of the peace accords. But the problem is not only the size of the armed forces, but their mystique. How do the armed forces train men for these sexual chores? Psychologists tell us that when children are molested by adults, they often grow up to molest other children. The government security forces scoop up their young recruits from the streets, sometimes at the age of thirteen or fourteen—just as they are becoming aware of their sexuality. There follows a brief interval during which recruits may be ransomed by their families. But the poor lack resources for the ransom of their young.

When this waiting period is over these young men undergo an indoctrination into the armed forces like the rituals of initiation developed by the S.S. They are brutalized. Often they are raped. Deserters say that sometimes this is done by older members of the service. Sometimes the penetration is simulated with a wooden object carved to resemble a large penis. It doesn't matter because the effects are the same. Shamed and humiliated, the young recruits can only reclaim their dignity through repetition. They convince themselves that what happened to them was insignificant by doing the same to others.

There is a purpose to all of this. One embraces a certain style in order to achieve a certain effect.

In El Salvador, stories of atrocities committed by government security troops and death squads spread by word-of-mouth. It is the attention to detail that captures people's imagination and leaves them shaking. But these stories are not fairy tales. They are punctuated with the hard evidence of corpses, mutilated flesh, splattered brains and eyewitnesses. Sadomasochistic killing creates terror. Terror creates passivity in the face of oppression. Why the need to control the peasants? A passive population is easy to control. Somebody has to pick the coffee and cotton and cut the sugar cane. These crops provide El Salvador with much of its foreign capital. Cash crops require large numbers of workers during certain seasons and create underemployment for the rest of the year. Idle peasants are dangerous, particularly when members of their families are hungry. They need to be controlled.

The social situation started to change in El Salvador after the Second Vatican Council. Joaquin Villalobos, a *commandante* of the FMLN, has written that the church's social teachings formed the base of El Salvador's revolutionary process. But what did the church actually *do* in El Salvador? It started programs for health education. It advocated land reform. It introduced literacy programs in many parishes. It trained lay leaders. But mostly, it listened to the poor. When somebody listens, the poor will talk. The church did not need to do much more. Once the poor discovered that the church was willing to listen, they started talking. Then they began to organize. That was when the recent wave of violence erupted.

The attorney general of El Salvador has accused the church of inciting violence. The church bears some responsibility, to be sure, but not the kind that the ARENA party is claiming. The church is culpable for listening to the poor and helping the poor to organize. And in El Salvador, that is a crime.

Albert Camus once wrote that the mind's deepest desire parallels our unconscious feeling in the face of the universe: "it is an insistence upon familiarity, an appetite for clarity." These attempts to understand often have consequences. North Americans have interpreted the Salvadoran reality through the template of North American experience and political categories. This has been true of both the "left" and the "right." But the fact is that North American categories simply do not fit the Salvadoran reality. The failed attempts of the American press and congress to describe and interpret events in El Salvador had grave consequences—incremental increases in aid, an escalation of the war and implicit support for the death squads.

Much of the analysis that came from American newspapers, radio and television broadcasts was simply ignorant. Some of it, however, was obscene. After the killing of the Jesuits, for example, some newspapers suggested that the Salvadoran "left" planned the massacre because of the political mileage they would make from this act. This is obscene. It would be irresponsible for the Salvadoran left not to cite this killing as evidence of ARENA's persistent political agenda for El Salvador, just as it would be immoral for us to forget the holocaust.

Other analysts suggested that the killing of the Jesuits was orchestrated by the left to inspire a reaction in the United States. This also is obscene.

These interpretations reflect a hermeneutic of guilt. The United States invested four billion dollars in El Salvador's war over the years of the Reagan and Bush administrations. Congress increased aid after rightists killed Archbishop Romero. It stopped aid for only two weeks after four American church-women were raped and killed. The 1989 military aid package for El Salvador was put through the Congress without requiring guarantees for human rights. Americans were guilty of supporting genocide and then attempting exculpation through an absolving act of interpretation. In this we may have committed a further obscenity.

It's time to become clean again.

CONCLUSION

Whom should we believe? To whom should we listen?

I suggest that we consider the words written by Archbishop Oscar Romero. On February 17, 1980, after learning of American intentions to send military aid and advisors to El Salvador, Romero wrote to then President Jimmy Carter, predicting that "instead of favoring greater justice and peace in El Salvador, your government's contribution will undoubtedly sharpen the injustice and the repression." Romero asked Carter "to forbid that military aid be given to the Salvadoran government." Five weeks later, Romero was dead—assassinated while saying mass. He fell "like the just ones" of the Hebrew scriptures, "between the sanctuary and the altar." His prophecy has proven chillingly true. His plea remains compellingly evident.

We should do as Romero did and listen to El Salvador's poor. Theirs is the only acceptable hermeneutic of death. El Salvador's truth can be found in rural huts and in city barrios after a day of back-breaking labor. During quiet moments, sitting with the poor and sharing a cup of sweet Salvadoran coffee, one couldn't help but notice that when the guerrillas were nearby people were relaxed. They may not have agreed with the guerrillas' politics. They may have wished they'd go away. But they were not terrorized by them.

But when the national guard, the army or the treasury police entered a village, the terror was palpable. This is the inescapable truth of El Salvador. It reduces to ash all other attempts to interpret this reality.

I saw this in Toñita's eyes every time she told her story to visiting delegations of North Americans. I found a key to interpreting the Salvadoran reality in Toñita's response to each query, "What do you want us to tell our government when we return home?"

"*No mas,*" she always said. "No more money for this war. Never again this death from the sky. We have had enough now..."

An earlier version of this chapter was published in America, *Vol. 162, No. 11, March 24, 1990.*

LIKE A THIEF IN THE NIGHT
A Salvadoran Soldier and His Community

The nature of making war is such that the relationship of a soldier to his society can become a decisive factor in the ultimate military outcome. This is especially true in a guerrilla war where both armies require the active support of the population, usually offered in the form of material assistance and military intelligence.

During its twelve year war, El Salvador's armed forces lacked the support of the general population. The isolation of individual soldiers and families of soldiers from the population-at-large greatly polarized Salvadoran society. The military's freedom to conduct the war irrespective of the values of the general population exacerbated this polarization and diminished the possibility for "winning" the peace through military intervention.

The song "When Johnny Comes Marching Home" expresses the need of soldiers to feel well-received when they return home from war, to be greeted with enthusiasm. The welcome that a society gives to its soldiers is a kind of absolution. It says: "Yes, you have killed, but you did this for us and so we forgive you." Salvadoran enlisted men did not return home to cheering throngs, but rather they returned home like thieves in the night. At leave-time, they slipped into their homes unobserved. When they went to the plaza, their friends avoided them. Soldiers and veterans remain incapable of distancing themselves from the acts of terror and random violence that typified the Salvadoran military's strategy. They are not loved; they are feared. They are not admired; they are loathed. Children do not gaze upon them as paragons of national service; rather, eyes are averted and glances cast down, hoping to avoid contact with the truth that lies behind false greetings and forced smiles.

I am a priest who works in El Salvador. My understanding of the relationship between people's support for a war and its outcome has been formed by my experience working in a community that includes

18

soldiers, the families of soldiers and supporters of the Salvadoran resistance, the FMLN, often all in the same family. The challenge I face, in post-war El Salvador, is to help reconcile families and communities torn apart by the war. The four stories presented here demonstrate the difficulty of this task.

The problem is deep. For years, before the outbreak of war in 1980 and throughout the recent conflict, the Salvadoran armed forces achieved internal solidarity by allowing officers and enlisted men to become wealthy through corruption and public extortion. Armed forces personnel have also been able to use their positions for private retribution and power, all under the mantle of public security. As the four testimonies reported below indicate, serious, deep reforms of the armed forces are required before the civilian population of El Salvador can reconcile itself to the armed forces and trust the armed forces' commitment to the peace accords.

THE EXTORTIONIST

Juan Martín was sixteen years old when he was "recruited" by the Salvadoran armed forces. On October 17, 1987 at eight in the evening, Juan left night school in Ciudad Delgado to return home. He was waiting at a bus stop with a group of friends when national guard soldiers appeared and forced Juan and ten others onto the back of a truck. The truck made one additional stop to recruit and then drove to the national guard headquarters in San Salvador. Some of the recruits had family connections with the military and so were excused from service. Others were able to bribe their way out. Juan Martín had neither connections nor money.

Juan went through the brutal and dehumanizing basic training. After a month his family was able to visit him at the military base. When Juan's mother returned home she reported to her friends that, although Juan was unhappy, he seemed to be adjusting. His education (two years of high school) and good health made him a likely candidate for one of the military units protecting government buildings in the city. Juan was unlikely to see much action on the war front, his mother said.

Juan Martín's first visit home came after he had been incorporated into a military company responsible for guarding commercial buildings owned by the retired officers association. Following military protocol in El Salvador, Juan did not wear his uniform when he returned home to the town of Apopa to visit his family. But his short, cropped hair and ersatz Ray-Ban sunglasses marked him clearly. Even without these tell-tale signs, Juan was well-known. Apopa is a small community and everybody knows who is and who is not a member of the armed forces.

Juan's home leave was for three days. He spent all of his first day in his parents' home. On the evening of the second day he arranged to meet a cousin at a small cafe that faces the plaza in Apopa. During this visit Juan learned his cousin had recently been involved in an automobile accident. The cousin's taxi had been destroyed when it collided with a truck. The police had dismissed any charges against the truck driver when it became evident that Juan's cousin had been drunk at the time of the accident.

Juan knew the truck driver. Without saying more, he told his cousin not to worry. Two weeks after Juan had returned to his base, this truck driver was apprehended by a national guard unit operating in the Apopa area. The man was brought to Juan's base. He reported later that he recognized Juan's voice during his "interrogation." The man was allowed to leave the base after two weeks of questioning, accusations and torture. The only condition of his release was that he immediately leave the country. His truck was seized as "evidence in a continuing investigation." It eventually found its way to Juan's cousin who sold it and is now driving a new taxi.

A THIEF IN THE NIGHT

Not all members of the armed forces are forcibly recruited. Some, like Carlos Gonzales, join for economic benefits. Carlos is somewhat typical of the young men who voluntarily join the armed forces.

Carlos' oldest brother died in San Vicente fighting with the FMLN. Two other brothers were captured by the army when they were fourteen and sixteen years old. At the time they were carrying beans and rice to the guerrillas. Carlos' brothers spent three years in the political prison at Mariona. At about the time that Carlos' brothers were sent to prison, the armed forces invaded his village. Carlos' grandparents and baby sister were burned alive in this invasion and his family forced to resettle in San Salvador. Carlos' mother, Paca, insulated her son from the political activities of his older brothers. He was her "baby," she said. She had given enough sons to the struggle. Let other mothers give their sons.

Paca sacrificed so that her youngest son could go to school. Carlos was spared the chore of selling fruit and candies in the early morning in the streets of San Salvador. When he grew up, Paca overlooked her son's indulgences of drinking beer and smoking marijuana. But beer and marijuana cost money—more than the few cents that Carlos was able to pilfer from his parents' earnings. Shortly after his seventeenth birthday, Carlos left his parents' house in San Salvador and returned to San Vicente where he enlisted in the fifth army brigade.

When he first disappeared from home, Carlos' mother and father thought that their son had been captured by the national guard. Then they learned from old neighbors in San Vicente that Carlos had joined the army. Ever since, Paca has suffered serious depression. Her son joined the same brigade that had killed her mother and father. When word spread that Carlos had joined the fifth army brigade, Paca told her neighbors that her son had been forcibly recruited. Now she admits that he joined the army, but she explains, "He did it because he needed money for his drug habit...I didn't know."

It was difficult for Carlos to maintain a relationship with his parents. While on his first home-leave, his father, Emilio, refused his son entry to the house. When Carlos' mother visited her son at the base in San Vicente, she did not tell her neighbors where she was going. "I'm going downtown for the day," she'd say, although everybody knew when Paca returned in the evening and cried all night that she'd been to see her son, the soldier.

After six months in the army, Carlos again attempted to visit his family. This time Emilio allowed his son to enter the house. I asked Emilio if he'd had a change of heart and forgiven his son.

"Do you know how my son returned home?" Emilio asked in response. "He came home like a thief in the night...like death. He took the bus from San Vicente. He arrived at the terminal and waited until dark. When the last bus was leaving for Santa Tecla he took it. He sat in the back and covered his face. He slipped into the house from the back and he left before the sun came up. If my son cannot forgive himself, how can I forgive him?"

Emilio continued: "It's not just the shame that my son has brought upon us, it's the danger as well. He told me—I don't know if this is true—that he is going to desert and cross the border into

Guatemala, Mexico and the United States. How can a man with a shaven head pass the border without a visa?

"But still, it's better to try and to fail than to continue this disgrace. If he deserts, they will come here to look for him. And so his brothers must leave as well, soon. I'll wait a while with my wife and when we're sure that they have left the country, we'll follow our sons."

This interview was conducted in 1990. Carlos never deserted. When peace was declared, he was one of the first to be decommissioned. He returned home but was asked to leave his village when he began inviting other young people in his community to share his newly found interest in cocaine.

THE "EAR"

Sister Bertha Chajito works in a middle class parish in San Salvador. The members of this parish represent El Salvador's whole political spectrum. Many were Christian Democrats who later joined the conservative ARENA party. The sons and daughters of Bertha's parish are likewise diverse, from radical supporters of the FMLN (some at the National University) to political activists for ARENA. The one place where all were welcomed and able to communicate was in the Catholic youth group organized by Sister Bertha.

"We were always a place for communication," Sister Bertha said. "One of our founding principles ten years ago was that without communication, we would never achieve peace. Throughout all these difficult years we have maintained that single value...until Roberto broke our covenant.

"Roberto had been a member of our group since 1984. In 1987 he left to study in the United States. He still maintained an active role in our group. He wrote when he was away and participated in our activities when he returned home. We all thought that he was studying engineering at a university in Atlanta.

"During the FMLN offensive in November 1989, El Salvador was placed under martial law. But things quieted down by mid-December and I spread the word that we were going to get together in the church hall for our annual Christmas gathering. Remember, I have worked with these young people for ten years and in that time we've developed some traditions. Naturally, I informed Roberto's parents so that he could join us if he came home in time. And he did.

"Miriam Gomez is another member of our youth group. She is a law student and volunteers with a human rights group in the capital. She also came to this Christmas gathering. When Miriam spotted Roberto, she walked right up to him and announced: 'I visited Mariona (the men's political prison) yesterday. I talked to Pablo and Saúl. Saúl couldn't talk much because of his broken jaw, but he could nod and shake his head.'"

Pablo and Saúl were also members of Sister Bertha's youth group. They are both law students at the National University and had become active in the labor movement. Sister Bertha says that they had often clashed with other young people in the parish over their political ideas, but still managed to remain friends with the whole group.

This young woman, Miriam, continued to confront Roberto: "They both say that you were their interrogator. They recognized your voice, even when you tried to disguise it. Pablo says he saw you when you left the interrogation room because they removed his hood too soon. He says you wore the uniform of the treasury police and that your questions were all based on things we had spoken of here, in the church."

Sister Bertha told me, "Roberto has a young face. When he lies, he blushes. When he is caught in a lie, he turns red. I'll never forget that moment. The other young people in the room, even those who share Roberto's political convictions, pulled away from him as if he were unclean. Roberto just stood in the midst of us all, turning red. Finally, he walked out of the room.

"Nobody said anything. I tried to visit Pablo and Saúl in prison, but when Miriam and I went to Mariona, they had been transferred to the treasury police headquarters."

Sister Bertha concluded: "I haven't seen Roberto since. I don't know what I'll say to him when I do. Probably nothing. The truth is, I'm afraid."

She also reports that, even with the cease fire, the young people in the parish no longer speak to one another. When they are brought together by some accident—a meeting, waiting at the bus stop, or leaving mass—they appear nervous and overly careful. Her young adult group has disbanded.

A MASS FOR THE DEAD

The national guard ordinarily did not assign its men to locales near their hometowns. Occasionally errors were made, however, and recruits found themselves involved in military campaigns close to home. Pedro Rivas is from Guazapa. He was forcibly recruited while in Apopa, trained at a military base in San Salvador and then assigned to a brigade working in the region of Guazapa. Pedro's superiors did not know this, as his identification papers indicated a false address in Apopa.

In early March 1990, the Salvadoran armed forces reinstituted Operation Phoenix, a military invasion of the Guazapa Hill which included aerial bombardment with incendiary and fragmentation bombs. After three days of heavy bombing, the combined troops of the national guard and army invaded the villages and cantons surrounding Guazapa in search of FMLN guerrillas. In effect, this meant looking for wounded men and women. The Salvadoran armed forces reasoned that, if people happened to be wounded in a military operation, they must be guerrillas.

Pedro Rivas' squad was ordered to search for "terrorists and terrorist supporters" in the small village of Aujuciote. Pedro was afraid that somebody from his home would identify him by calling out his name or speaking with him. If his captain learned that Aujuciote was his home and that he had false identity papers, he would be held as a suspected infiltrator.

The fact was that Pedro knew full well who was and who was not an FMLN supporter in this hamlet of twenty houses. Pedro did not speak to his brothers, his sister or other relatives and friends he saw in the streets of Aujuciote. He did not visit his father and mother. He hardened his face and waited for the helicopters to arrive to take him, his comrades and their prisoners away.

The national guard invasion of Aujuciote was typically brutal. They knocked down doors they could have opened. A young girl was raped the first night the *guardia* was in Aujuciote. A few "suspected sympathizers" were located. One had an old gunshot scar on his shoulder. Pedro Rivas knew this man had received his scar as a result of a domestic quarrel years ago, but said nothing for fear of revealing himself. Pedro knew that the other suspects taken by the *guardia* could just as likely have been wounded during the bombing of Guazapa while looking for firewood (as two claimed) or while cutting banana leaves for sale in the Apopa market, as three others claimed.

At five o'clock in the evening of the second day of this campaign, a small delegation of townspeople approached Pedro's captain to request permission to hold a prayer service for a deceased member of their community. Such services are common in El Salvador and are held either nine days or forty days after the death. The captain had not encountered any difficulties in this operation and was in a generous mood. He granted permission on the condition that the service end by six-thirty. "That will not be a problem, sir," the spokesman from Aujuciote said. "We need very little time to pray." To ensure that his orders were obeyed, the captain assigned four of his men, including Pedro Rivas, to monitor the prayer service.

Imagine Pedro's surprise when his family and neighbors entered the plaza, carrying aloft his framed confirmation class photograph, draped in black. The procession passed in front of Pedro. The photograph was placed on a table adorned with flowers. Prayers and songs for Pedro's deceased soul were offered and Pedro's mother cried and cried and cried while her son witnessed his own funeral.

When the people of Aujuciote completed their service, they filed past Pedro Rivas once again. None of them lifted their eyes to look into his. His mother did not stop to speak to her son. Even in El Salvador, one doesn't stop to talk with a dead man.

CONCLUSION

For the past one hundred and fifty years the power of Salvadoran armed forces personnel over the civilian population has been absolute and arbitrary. This included the colonels who planned El Salvador's wars and common soldiers like Juan Martín who fought them. A simple grudge, a minor altercation or an accident can still earn the wrath of the military and that wrath may mean death. This was particularly evident during the war when the military's lack of support from among the general population heightened the armed forces' need for internal solidarity. Lacking support from the society at large, soldiers supported one another. This remains the case today, and perhaps more so as the armed forces have come under public, international scrutiny. The feeling is that when one soldier has a problem, all of his comrades have a problem. In a country where a rumor can damn, it is easy to transform a grudge into an accusation and on that basis condemn a man or woman to prison or death. Most Salvadoran families have been victimized by the armed forces in this fashion. This is well-known and documented. For the majority of people in El Salvador, the armed forces represent death and not the more laudatory virtues one hears broadcast over the armed forces radio network: God, patriotism, liberty, national unity.

The most contentious point in the peace negotiations between the FMLN and the government of El Salvador was the reform of the armed forces. Until serious reforms are made of the armed forces, these abuses will continue. But at a deeper level, the armed forces cannot be reformed to somehow become the solution to El Salvador's problems. The source of El Salvador's problems lies in the lack of justice and the prostitution of the democratic process by the far-right to maintain their power over the vast majority of the people. Until this problem is addressed, the armed forces will remain alienated from the interests of the people. Alienated from its national society, an army soon becomes a law unto itself and the cycle of violence and repression continues.

TORTURED INTO THE ARMY
Recruitment into the Salvadoran Armed Forces

Considering the atrocious abuses committed by the Salvadoran military against the poor, one might wonder how the armed forces of El Salvador were able to maintain a standing force of 65,000 troops throughout the decade of the 1980s. The answer lay in El Salvador's system of "recruiting," a euphemism for selective (against the poor), forced military impressment. The Salvadoran constitution mandates military service for men between the ages of eighteen and thirty. The constitution also states that secondary legislation will stipulate the rules under which this mandate is to be carried out. But no such secondary legislation exists. With the exception of a few upper-class youths who enter the military academies, El Salvador's wealthy and middle class studiously avoid military service.

"Recruits," young men from poor urban and rural communities, were regularly seized off the streets, taken off buses, emptied from playing fields. Once a month, often on the first of the month, military patrols scoured El Salvador's poor city neighborhoods and rural villages in search of new soldiers, often seizing fourteen and fifteen year old boys. Bus stops near high schools and colleges were favorite haunts for these "recruitments," as were church youth-group meetings and soccer games. Early weekday mornings were also considered ideal opportunities to search for recruits as young men lined up at bus stops on their way to school or work.

The military cordoned these areas and then separated the young men from other bystanders. Identity papers were checked and the youths forced into the backs of trucks and driven to a military barracks far from their homes. Processing draftees in military bases far from their homes has a threefold effect. It disorients and demoralizes the young men. It makes it more difficult for families to locate them. It makes it difficult for the young men to flee.

The recruiting campaigns of the Salvadoran armed forces exhib-

27

ited a definite pattern after the November 1989 offensive mounted by the Salvadoran resistance, the FMLN. The communities in the province of San Salvador which supported the FMLN during its 1989 offensive were Soyapango, Zacamil, Mejicanos, Ciudad Delgado and Apopa. On Thursday, March 29, 1990 the military recruited sixty young men from Soyapango. Forty recruits were taken from Zacamil and Mejicanos. Fifty young men from Ciudad Delgado and an additional fifty from the Apopa area were pressed into military service on this one day. Others were taken from the poor barrios that line the river running through San Salvador. In all, twenty trucks each carrying thirty young men were seen heading up the northern highway to the army base at El Paraiso in the province of Chalatenango. This was the final ignominy; the communities which had resisted the armed forces in November were forced to fill the armed forces' quota of fresh recruits in March.

Military recruitment was an issue that the FMLN attempted, successfully, to introduce as part of the peace negotiations. For a time, the Salvadoran armed forces are demobilizing its brigades and have no need to recruit. But when the time comes again to recruit, the armed forces will either have to reform in such a way that it can become a volunteer force, or else create a classless draft system. Both options demand radical change. The testimonies offered below present yet another view of the breach between the Salvadoran armed forces and the people of El Salvador. This breach can only be closed through serious reform of the armed forces.

TORTURED INTO THE ARMY

José Llantana lives in a small resettlement community in Soyapango. José's father was killed in the military invasion of Chalatenango in 1982. José, his mother and baby sister fled to San Salvador where they sought refuge in the camp at the archdiocesan seminary and later in a resettlement community in Soyapango. José works in a factory in San Salvador. He leaves his house every morning at 5:30. After working all day, he attends night school from 5 to 8 P.M. José was waiting for a bus at 5:45 A.M. when the military truck pulled into sight. Before José could flee, he was caught in a military cordon and forced into the back of a truck. The truck made two additional stops before entering the national guard fort in San Salvador at 7:30 A.M.

José and twenty-five other young men were kept on this truck throughout the day. After an hour they were joined by another truck holding thirty additional young men from Soyapango. When the caravan reached its full complement of twenty trucks—at about 5:30 in the afternoon—all of these vehicles left for the army base at El Paraiso.

When the convoy passed a small cafeteria on the northern highway a neighbor spotted José. This neighbor later informed José's mother that her son had been "recruited." By seven in the evening Mrs. Llantana had contacted the priest in Soyapango. The priest drafted a letter to the commander of the El Paraiso army base explaining that José was an only son and provider for his family and pleaded for his release from military service. The following morning, José's mother obtained additional letters from José's boss at the factory and another from the archdiocese of San Salvador. By one o'clock in the afternoon, Mrs. Llantana was on a bus to El Paraiso to seek her son's release.

The day before, José and six hundred other recruits had made the long journey to El Paraiso. Upon entering the base at ten o'clock at night, they were herded off the trucks and forced into five lines. The young men, lacking any military experience, faltered in formation. This earned them sharp rebukes, rifle butts in their stomachs and other abuse. José later reported that "the captain who ordered us off the truck seemed to pick out a few guys to make into an example. Their posture was no worse than the rest of us, but they were beaten in front of us all until they were unconscious. I think one of them might have died. His skull was split and I saw his brains oozing out of his head."

This exhibition had the desired effect. "I don't think the lines got any straighter, but they scared us. You could smell the urine and the feces. People were so scared they actually urinated in their pants.

"The five lines were made to turn," José continued to recall, "and we approached a table where our identity papers were to be checked. This is when I really got scared. I don't have a *cedula* (official identification papers) because we are from the province of Chalatenango but now live in the Province of San Salvador. I have a voting card, but I forgot to carry it with me that morning."

José was fortunate. The soldiers had grown lax in their effort to process the high volume of recruits. The sergeants at the tables only asked for name, age and residence, without demanding proof of identity. José and his fellow recruits were then marched onto another parade ground lit by a circle of fires. By this time, José had been on his feet since 5:30 in the morning. He had not eaten or had anything to drink. He had been subjected to exposure of the sun and to the physical abuse of the army. "Next, they had us stand at attention while a colonel mounted a small stage and gave us a talk about serving our country in the armed forces. He told us how fortunate we were to have been 'chosen.' He said that the war against the communist terrorists had ruined the economy, but as recruits we would be taken care of and even earn enough to send money home. When he finished talking, we were told to lay down and sleep.

"But who could sleep? I heard moaning. Some guys were crying. The soldiers walked among us and if they heard anyone making a sound, they kicked the person until he was unconscious. Two guys were caught talking. They were taken out kicking and screaming. We heard their screams throughout the night.

"I remembered somebody at the shop where I work saying, 'They can kick you, hit you, put a bag over your head (a form of torture, often accompanied by severe beating) but they can't make you enlist. You have to sign your name or make your mark on the enlistment paper.' I remembered this.

"The next morning—I don't know what time it was but it was still dark—we were awakened by the kicking of our guards. Then the guards ordered us to form five lines in alphabetical groupings. This confused things because not everybody knew how to spell his name. Those who didn't—they were mostly from the countryside—didn't know which line to enter. The officers went among us and the guys who were in the wrong line were beaten until they found the right place to stand. One guy tried three lines before he found his place. And his name began with 'A.'

"When I got to the table this time, the official asked my name. He looked through his stack of papers for my recruitment paper and told me to sign my name. I asked him what the paper said. He told me, 'It says that you agree to serve the fatherland in the armed forces for two years and to obey the laws of the country relating to military behavior.'

"I answered that I didn't want to be in the army. He called me a communist. I said that I was not a communist, but that I needed to work close to my home to help my mother. He didn't say anything else to me. He just called one of the soldiers and said, 'This one's a terrorist. Take him away.'

"I was brought into a building and an empty cement bag was tied over my head. They started to beat me. I think they used a piece of bamboo, but I'm not sure. 'This is how we take care of terrorists,' they shouted. I screamed for them to stop.

"When they stopped, I could hear others being beaten. I heard screams and soldiers shouting abuse: 'This is how we take care of communists.'

"My biggest problem now was thirst. I had not had anything to drink in over twenty-four hours. The sun was hot, but worse, I had inhaled the dry cement from the bag over my head and my mouth and throat were cracked from dryness.

"Do you know that when your mouth is completely dry like this, you can't scream? It's true. They continued to beat me but I couldn't scream or cry out.

"I don't know how much time passed...it felt like a long time, but I really don't know. After a while, a lieutenant came into the room where I was being held and ordered the bag removed. He asked me if I was ready to join the armed forces or if I wanted to suffer the same fate as my 'terrorist friends.'

"All I could think about was that I could disappear and nobody would know the difference. I asked the lieutenant for water. He nodded to one of the soldiers and I was given a cup of water. He then repeated his question and I said 'I am not a terrorist, but I can't join the armed forces because I have to take care of my mother and sister.' He shook his head and told the soldiers to continue their 'interrogation.'

"I was beaten three more times that day before I passed out. When I woke up the next day I was in a room with maybe thirty other guys. All of us were bloody. We all had huge lumps on our faces, arms and backs. One guy had lost an eye. It was still hanging from its socket, punctured and bleeding. Later that morning the lieutenant who had interrogated me came into this room and announced, 'You are all being held on suspicion of aiding the terrorists. If any one of you wishes to plead for the forgiveness of your country, the armed forces offers this final opportunity to do so.'

"I was ready to enlist. Do you know what stopped me? The guy with the punctured eye. He was lying on the floor. He lifted himself on his elbow and made a motion to sign the recruitment papers. The lieutenant just laughed. He didn't refuse him. He didn't help this guy stand. He just laughed and called for the other soldiers stationed by the door to join him in this bitter joke. It was his hideous laughter that gave me the strength not to sign the recruitment papers.

"The lieutenant left and after another five or six hours a

sergeant came into this room and told us that if we didn't want to serve the fatherland, we could leave. Some couldn't leave because of their injuries. I was sure this was a trick, that they were going to kill us as we left the base. But they didn't kill us. I didn't have enough money to pay for the trip back to San Salvador, but the bus driver let me ride for free. I got home at about ten o'clock at night."

José's mother had also spent the day at El Paraiso. She had presented her letters to an officer at El Paraiso's gate and was promptly told that none of the recruits were to be released from military duty. The road in front of the base was filled with crying mothers, anxious fathers and relatives searching for lost sons and brothers. This recruitment had been so large that word had quickly spread throughout the poor neighborhoods of San Salvador that the young men had been taken to El Paraiso. The atmosphere outside the base was desperate. Mothers held up photographs of their sons to the soldiers on the parapets and asked for information regarding their whereabouts. Some young women—sisters and girlfriends of the recruits—tried flirting with the guards to gain access to the base. But neither entreaties nor promises worked that day and the family members returned home in despair.

I was with José's mother throughout the day and I was with her when her son walked into their small home that night. José's mother did not stop crying from happiness for days. José's story is not typical. José was lucky. He just happened to overhear a co-worker remark that military recruitment in El Salvador is not official until the recruit signs his name. This is not the case, but this misinformation gave José the strength to resist. José was also physically strong enough to resist abuse that most human beings would find unbearable.

RECOVERING HIS PRIDE

When Miguel Chavez was drafted by the Salvadoran armed forces, he was unable to resist his recruiters. "I couldn't stand it when they started beating me," Miguel told me. "I didn't want to be in the army, but I couldn't resist them either."

Miguel's family is from Zacatecoluca. At the time of his "recruitment" his older brother and sister were FMLN combatants in San Vicente. When Miguel was recruited, he was brought to the army base in San Miguel, far from his home and family. "I went through basic training," Miguel attests. "It was difficult, but not as bad as the recruitment. The lieutenant in charge of my platoon was even friendly with us. Still, I couldn't forget how they had treated us like animals.

"After two months, we were granted a leave. Before we were allowed to leave the base, however, they shaved our heads again. This was to prevent us from leaving the country for Guatemala. I was ashamed. I almost didn't go home. But I did.

"It was difficult. My friends didn't want to talk with me. They stopped by to joke about my hair. But I only had two days home and I didn't want to spend it talking about my haircut."

Miguel continued, "On the second day of my leave my brother Saúl came home. This was very difficult for me. I'd always looked up to Saúl and when I was a boy I wanted to be like him. And here I was in the armed forces while he's a guerrilla! He was careful. He asked how I liked being in the army. I got more and more angry with him. Finally I screamed, 'Saúl, listen to me. I didn't join. I was recruited. They hit us. I think they may have killed some of the recruits. I want to leave the country, but how can I leave like this?'

"The next morning—very early, it was still dark—Saúl came to my bedside. He told me that he knew I had not betrayed him. He told me to be patient. He was leaving to join his squad, he said, but he would return and talk with me the next time I was home on leave.

"I didn't see Saúl for six months after that, even though I came home every month. Finally, when I was home for the Holy Week truce, Saúl visited with a *compañero* (a fellow guerrilla) from San Miguel. The three of us talked into the night. This *compañero* was an intelligence agent for the FMLN. He asked me questions about troop strength and how our patrols were deployed. Then he explained how my military unit included FMLN sympathizers and how I could help the struggle from inside the army.

"I never learned who these others were, but I helped the FMLN in a number of ways. The quartermaster corps is very lax in the armed forces. We're able to draw supplies—grenades and bullets—without too much trouble. I drew many supplies and left these in two different spots where they were picked up. My outside contact with the FMLN told me that, once I had proven myself on an operation, I'd learn the names of others in my company working with the FMLN. He said that the FMLN even worked with some officers, although I never learned which ones."

As I spoke with Miguel at his mother's house in Zacatecoluca, I must have exhibited some skepticism. He sensed my suspicion and so interpreted his own behavior for me. "If I had not been recruited, I would not have worked for the *Frente* (the FMLN). I believe in the struggle, just as my brother and sister do, but I'm not political. I had a job. I was learning auto mechanics and I was happy. It was the way that we were taken and treated that made me rebel. My FMLN contact knew this about me. He joked with me sometimes: 'You have no political conviction,' he would say. I laughed when he said this, but it's true. I have no political convictions, but I do have my pride."

LIVING WITH KNOWING THAT...

Antonio Geronimo was not forcibly recruited. He had a good job in an auto repair shop but few prospects for advancement. Antonio's unhappiness lay in the fact that there was little more he could learn about engines in this small shop and he wanted to learn much more. Antonio's intellectual curiosity, together with a completely apolitical outlook on life, brought him into the Salvadoran air force as a mechanic.

After completing his basic training, Antonio was sent to a special school at Ilopango military airport to learn jet engine repair and maintenance. After completing his apprenticeship he was assigned to a crew responsible for the care of the A-37 Dragonfly attack aircraft at Ilopango. "I liked my work. The pay was good. I learned a lot. I thought that after a few years I might be able to get a job at the airport working for TACA (El Salvador's national airline). I didn't participate in any military operations so I was not responsible for any atrocities."

This is how Antonio thinks. Yet he knows the A-37s he kept in such fine repair were used on February 11, 1990 to attack a refugee resettlement at Corral de Piedra in the province of Chalatenango. But Antonio's sense of moral responsibility ends with his wrench. He didn't drop the bombs so he doesn't feel responsible for the death of the innocent civilians killed in bombing raids. What did disrupt Antonio's clearly delineated categories was the infiltration of some FMLN supporters into his unit at Ilopango. "We all knew who they were," he reported. "And it was hard living with them, knowing that while I repaired engines, some of these others destroyed them. I once returned to one of the repair sheds to finish working on an engine overhaul I had begun and caught one of these guys pouring sugar into the fuel line. I caught him in the act. This usually didn't happen, but I'd returned unexpectedly. He looked at me. I looked at him. He continued pouring sugar into the plane and I watched. When he was done, he nodded to me; I nodded to him and then I started the job of cleaning the engine."

When I asked Antonio why he didn't report this man to the authorities at Ilopango, he replied: "I'm not political. I just wanted to learn about airplane engines. Base security wasn't my responsibility."

Antonio Geronimo represents the best the armed forces could expect to find among its enlisted men. He pursued a career, quite independently of the political goals of El Salvador's war. But while Antonio represents the best, he was a poor excuse for a soldier. He was only faithful to his career goals. He even lacked loyalty to his comrades at Ilopango whose lives depended on the attention he gave to their airplanes and helicopters. Antonio admits to having felt some confusion at the presence of FMLN infiltrators within his squadron, but this confusion never prompted him to ask questions or to take a stand. If anything, it strengthened his resolve to ignore the contradictions inherent in El Salvador's civil war.

CONCLUSION

"Torture" is a serious word, and like all serious words it should be used sparingly. That said, the fact is that during the twelve year civil war, young Salvadoran men were given two options: to be tortured (possibly to death) or join the armed forces. The ethical problems inherent in El Salvador's military recruitment are self-evident. Still, one must be careful about judging one society's values with the standards of another. "You Americans don't live under the threat of communism," Salvadoran military officers are frequently heard to say. "You can't judge us because you don't share our history." Whether or not this is a good argument, it often silences criticism.

What defies this apologetic is the practical argument against such methods. Forced recruitment undermines morale in the armed forces. Limiting recruitment to the poor sectors of Salvadoran society proves to the poor that the military exists to protect limited interests— those of the wealthy. The low morale and poor performance of El Salvador's ground troops forced the military to rely on the air force in its campaign against the Salvadoran resistance. An air force can be used for support in a guerrilla war, but it cannot win the war. Worse, the over-use of the air force caused an increase in civilian deaths and

further alienated the civilian population from the military and government.

As military theorists throughout history have attested, one index
of an army's strength is the morale of its troops. Brilliant strategizing
and superior firepower are alone insufficient to win a war. Soldiers
must desire to win. El Salvador's military recruits never exhibited such
a desire.

The testimonies presented here continue to raise important
questions for North Americans, particularly in light of the negotiated
peace accords.

—Should North Americans support a military structure that
favors the interests of the wealthy classes in a country where the
wealthy are themselves unwilling to support the military, either
through service to their armed forces or with taxes?

—Should we support a military establishment which has consis-
tently undermined the democratic process and denied due process to
its citizens?

—Should we support a military establishment that presents torture as the alternative to military service?

These questions are no less important given the peace accord
signed on January 16, 1992 between the guerrilla force and the government of El Salvador. For North Americans they constitute the
most important decisions we need to make about El Salvador—indeed
in terms of our relations to all our hemispheric neighbors—if we are to
play a role as partners to peace.

DOMINGO MONTERROSA
A Myth of Power, a Parable of Vindication

Myths express a people's values. The heroes of myths—the kind of men and women a society chooses to lionize—tell much about a people's aspirations, their goals and what they are willing to sacrifice to attain their goals. Myths are often religious, but not exclusively. The corpus of myths generated by the German national socialist and Italian fascist parties in this century exemplify political myth-making. Sometimes myths draw from traditional legends, images and metaphors, as did Nazi myths of nature. Others use historical events, usually distorting these, to revitalize national values. The Italian fascists' glorification of the Roman empire exemplifies this kind of myth-making. In both instances, myths serve a social function. They draw on cultural materials and history to establish a particular ideology within a cosmic plan.

Parable is a literary and speech form employed in religious as well as in secular teaching. Fundamentally, parables are stories which compare two realities. Parables draw from everyday experience to shed light on the interior life. Parables often use surprise, paradox and irony to lead listeners to conclusions that would otherwise remain hidden. While they seldom purport to communicate history, as historical myths claim, parables draw from historical sources. For example, the parable of the Good Samaritan would be unintelligible if one lacks a prior understanding of the historical conflict between the Samaritans and Jews.

The armed forces of El Salvador and the Salvadoran resistance, the FMLN, both drew from the life of a now-deceased colonel, Domingo Monterrosa, as a source of myth and parable. The "facts" surrounding Monterrosa's life are less important than the way these facts were interpreted by the Salvadoran armed forces and by the FMLN. Their conflicting interpretations reveal much about the values and ideas behind the twelve year struggle to gain control of this tiny country.

The legends surrounding the like of Monterrosa are particularly important to "demythologize." More than a simple instance of propagandizing by the powerful in an effort to spread a military ideology, Domingo Monterrosa has achieved hero status among the "reform" elements of the Salvadoran military. Considering the facts attending to his life and the emphasis given to certain aspects of his life by the "Domingo Monterrosa (reformist) brigade," it is difficult to invest much hope in the self-reform of the Salvadoran armed forces.

DOMINGO MONTERROSA AND MOZOTE

Resistance movements require the active support of the civilian population. The Salvadoran military's scorched-earth policy of the early 1980s attempted to eliminate this support. It received support from the Reagan White House and the United States embassy in San Salvador. U.S. intelligence officers guaranteed the necessary logistical assistance, aerial intelligence and training for the dreaded Atlacatl battalion, which headed this effort.

The FMLN coordinated with civilian leadership in the "liberated" zones in efforts to evacuate non-combatants during military invasions. When the FMLN received information of an invasion in progress, they relayed this information to their civilian counterparts who supervised the *guinda*, or flight of the people. While the people fled, the FMLN combatants resisted the invading army until they themselves were able to melt into their mountainous strongholds.

On December 15, 1981 the FMLN received word of an invasion force leaving the headquarters of the Atlacatl battalion in San Miguel. Its destination was the villages around Mozote in Morazan. The Atlacatl battalion was under the command of Colonel Domingo Monterrosa. Monterrosa had gained infamy among Salvadoran peasants for his slaughter of civilians during military campaigns. He had often been accused of direct participation in the torture-interrogation of FMLN captives and their alleged supporters.

The FMLN warned the residents of Mozote to flee. But with a few exceptions, they chose to remain in their homes. Unlike most people in Morazan, the inhabitants of Mozote were predominantly fundamentalist-Protestants, members of the ultra-conservative Assemblies of God, which blesses the efforts of the Salvadoran military. Assemblies of God churches decry the threat of communism they believe the FMLN represents. The church prohibits its members from becoming involved in anti-government demonstrations and encourages them to inform on "local agitators." Mozote was somewhat typical of communities where the Assemblies of God is active. The people offered no support to the FMLN combatants and so the FMLN largely ignored Mozote. After its warning was heard and rejected, the FMLN combatants left Mozote to its fate.

The soldiers of the Atlacatl battalion arrived by helicopter at about seven in the morning. The people of Mozote did not run for cover, believing themselves to be "the righteous of God." The men of the Atlacatl battalion disembarked from their helicopters and rounded up all the residents of Mozote, separating the men from the women and children. The men they crowded into the church. The women and children were herded into the homes. No pretense of interrogation was made. No effort was made to separate alleged FMLN supporters from the general population of Mozote. The officers simply ordered the killing to begin. A special site was selected for the execution of the women and children. Their bodies were to be burned.

These women and children were led in groups of twelve to a small ravine. There, the women were raped before being lined up and shot, their bodies heaped onto a pile for eventual burning. When the line of victims faltered or the crying children threatened to disrupt the orderliness of the execution, Colonel Monterrosa's subalterns gave sharp orders to set things right with the prod of their bayonets. One woman managed to find cover under a pile of loose brush in the ravine. From her hiding place this single survivor of the Mozote massacre watched in horror as the Atlacatl battalion continued to lead women and children into the ravine and kill them. This same survivor later reported how some of the small children had not died as a result of their gunshot wounds and were heard crying out as they burned alive on the funeral pyre.

Monterrosa took little care for the bodies of the men. Many of the male bodies were discovered in the village, victims of machine gun execution and slit throats. Young boys were found hung from the trees. Many others, not included in the initial roundup, were burned alive in their homes. The army retreated in their helicopters, radioing ahead that the operation had been a success and that no injuries or fatalities had occurred.

The FMLN's *Radio Venceremos* immediately broadcast news of the event across El Salvador. It branded Monterrosa "The monster of Mozote" and publicly challenged the government and military to condemn the massacre. When the government and military refused to distance themselves from Monterrosa, *Radio Venceremos* intensified its attack. The colonel responded by promising to put *Radio Venceremos* out of commission, "to destroy its Cuban-backed installations" and "to bring to justice the terrorists who assault the people of El Salvador with this continual barrage of lies." Over the next four years the enmity between Colonel Monterrosa and *Radio Venceremos* intensified. The FMLN maintained its condemnation of the colonel. This had little influence, however, and Monterrosa was promoted to the command of the third brigade based in the province of San Miguel.

On October 23, 1984 Colonel Monterrosa's intelligence team reported a sighting of *Radio Venceremos'* portable broadcast facility near Mozote. If the armed forces moved quickly, they could eliminate an important element in the FMLN's public communication effort. Monterrosa invited his successor in the Atlacatl battalion, Colonel Jerson Calicto, two additional colonels, other officers, his military chaplain and a delegation from COPREFA, the government journalist pool, to join his foray to eliminate *Radio Venceremos.* Monterrosa's squad discovered what appeared to be a large transmitter and camouflaged broadcast tower. No FMLN combatants were seen, nor were any of *Radio Venceremos'* crew captured.

Still, Colonel Monterrosa was elated. The seizure of hardware was perhaps more important than the capture of prisoners. The FMLN had no difficulty recruiting personnel; its lack of access to military hardware and radio equipment was its Achilles' heel. Monterrosa ordered the transmitter loaded into his helicopter. He invited his guests to join him in San Miguel for a small victory celebration and departed, leaving his subordinates to scour the area for evidence of additional FMLN activities.

Colonel Monterrosa's helicopter was airborne for only a few minutes when the bomb hidden within the fake transmitter exploded, killing him and all fourteen members of his party. The impact of the blast and the explosion caused by the burning fuel sent pieces of helicopter and body parts scattering over Mozote. All the bodies were destroyed. But the lack of a corpse did nothing to diminish the pageantry of Monterrosa's funeral. With this fiery death the colonel entered Salvadoran military mythology.

THE MONTERROSA MYTH

Every morning *Radio Cuscatlan,* the official armed forces radio station, broadcasts "The Ballad of Domingo Monterrosa."

Our Colonel Domingo Monterrosa
Had no fear of the subversives

When he went to Morazan
The subversives were dispersed.
But they prepared their treachery well.
Lacking the courage
To confront Colonel Monterrosa directly,
They sought another way to take his life
    —in a helicopter of fire.

By this criminal act,
They stole the life of our fallen comrade.

Radio Cuscatlan could be named "I Remember Colonel Monterrosa" so frequent are the references to the former Atlacatl battalion chief. The radio seldom mentions the Mozote "invasion" (as it is euphemistically characterized at times). Rather, former comrades-in-arms of the colonel, who are guests on *Radio Cuscatlan,* recall his personal commitment to his men and how he shared the dangers of the campaign with them. This is significant for a number of reasons.

First and foremost, a commander's presence on the front lines belies the Salvadoran foot-soldiers' stereotype of the fattened officer calculating how many of his men are expendable in a military campaign. A ranking officer who goes to battle with his men has proven his concern for their well-being and the confidence that all that can be done to guarantee their safety has been done. Such an officer is bound to be regarded as a hero in El Salvador.

In El Salvador front-line participation carried added weight among enlisted men and junior officers. These subordinates were often held responsible for atrocities ordered by higher authorities. In 1989-1990 the Salvadoran military was in the midst of a crisis created by the arrest of the killers of six Jesuit priests and two women in November 1989. Colonel Benavides, who was found guilty for ordering this assassination, was held "prisoner" in comfortable lodgings, occasionally venturing out to a military hotel near the Pacific coast. Meanwhile the two junior officers and enlisted men who carried out his orders languished in prison. The court recognized that all evidence pointed to complicity in this crime by higher authorities, but none were charged. One of the lieutenants and all enlisted men were eventually freed. The expectation is that Colonel Benavides and the other lieutenant will be granted amnesty.

Monterrosa was an exception to the rule of commanding officers sending their subordinates to do the dirty work. If dirty work was to be done, Monterrosa wanted to be in on the action. "He never assigned us tasks he was not himself willing to accomplish," one former colleague recalled on *Radio Cuscatlan*. "The colonel always told his junior officers that the war would be lost if the high command refused to bloody its hands in active combat against the communist terrorists." "Monterrosa was himself a pillar of El Salvador's new order," the radio commentator added to these remembrances. "His legend lives on in the memory of the armed forces and in the trembling of the communists when they are confronted by the valiant soldiers of the Atlacatl battalion, in whose veins courses the blood of the Lion of San Miguel (Monterrosa)."

Through its myth-making, the Salvadoran military has attempted to transform campaigns that were little more than massacres of defenseless peasants into epic battles. Men like Colonel Domingo Monterrosa become heroes in such myths, and their actions—well-known to the general population—become sanctified within the military. The Monterrosa myth has significant official support beyond the radio station. Recruits, especially to the Atlacatl battalion, were made to sing Monterrosa's praises as they undertook basic training. Soldiers chanted slogans as they exercised or as they went through the obstacle course, for example, "Monterrosa lives—communists tremble," or "The Lion of San Miguel—the spirit of victory." Monterrosa's military tactics are studied by officers-in-training. Even though the Mozote massacre took place in 1981, the Salvadoran military can hardly be said to have distanced itself from this event, as the lionizing of Monterrosa clearly indicates.

Monterrosa's name is similar to the Spanish word *mentirosa* which means "liar." For the majority of Salvadorans, the official, post-mortem efforts to transform Monterrosa into a larger-than-life hero are a great lie. They cannot distract people from the fact of his bloody role at Mozote or in other massacres. A popular Salvadoran hymn to Oscar Romero, assassinated archbishop of San Salvador, includes the words: "History will not be silenced." The history of the "Mozote invasion" will not be silenced. The people of Mozote went meekly to their deaths. But, in death, the voices of Mozote's dead reach beyond the grave and make a lie of the official efforts to transform the Monster of Mozote into the Lion of San Miguel. Regardless of the consequences of the Salvadoran cease-fire, the historical truth of Mozote promises to ring louder than the ballads played over *Radio Cuscatlan*.

THE MONTERROSA PARABLE

Among El Salvador's poor, and particularly among supporters of the FMLN, Monterrosa's life and death is recounted as a parable. A parable is a type of story that includes elements of irony and surprise. In parables, the lowly find justice, the weak discover power and the powerful are brought down. Parables are told not as history, but as lessons in morality. The Monterrosa parable is invariably linked to his participation in the Mozote massacre. The implication is that God sometimes intervenes in history to reverse the fortunes of the powerful and the lowly. Like the parables of the Christian gospels, these moments of intervention foreshadow future events. Among El Salvador's poor this means the eventual outcome of the war in which the lowly will be vindicated and the powerful chastised.

The elements to this parable are simple: As a military leader Monterrosa represented the most reactionary clique of the Salvadoran armed forces. He completely disregarded civilians in his pursuit of the FMLN, and when he suspected communities of collaboration with the FMLN, he massacred them. Monterrosa was accused by *Radio Venceremos* of his crimes. He developed an all-consuming hatred for *Radio Venceremos*. "It was *Radio Venceremos* that accused the Monster of Mozote," one elderly woman recalled. "Monterrosa became obsessed by his accuser. His obsession drove him to his death. He pursued his obsession beyond all reason." A former FMLN combatant recalled meetings where Monterrosa's death was planned. "We baited Monterrosa. We knew this man's weakness; it was his pride. Monterrosa was hungry. The trap was sweetened and he snatched the bait. It was *Radio Venceremos* that killed Monterrosa. He was killed by the truth."

In Morazan, October 23, the day of Monterrosa's death, is celebrated as a local holiday. These celebrations are more than a remembrance of deliverance. Like the Jewish celebration of Passover and the Christian feast of Easter, October 23 is a day of promise of future salvific acts. In this respect, the Monterrosa parable is eschatological. It promises to repeat itself and foreshadows further justice for the poor.

Not only was Monterrosa killed, but his successor in the hated Atlacatl battalion was killed in the helicopter explosion as well. Salvadoran story-tellers interpret this death as evidence of God's vengeance against the battalion that carried out Monterrosa's orders. The implication of the parable is that just as the Atlacatl battalion will suffer for its crimes, so also will the United States which created this battalion. The Atlacatl's infamy has grown since Mozote. In addition to Mozote, it was responsible for the massacre at the Gualsinga River. In 1989 the Atlacatl killed the six Jesuit priests and two women domestics at the University of Central America. It is no wonder that the FMLN insisted throughout the peace negotiations that the Atlacatl battalion be eliminated as a condition for the cease fire.

For the poor of El Salvador, and particularly for FMLN supporters, Monterrosa's life and death form a modern parable. Through parables, historical events take on the aura of God's miraculous intervention in human affairs. Parables, like myths, tend to sanctify and bless human actions, in this case the killing of Domingo Monterrosa.

CONCLUSION

Both myth and parable involve some degree of distortion. Myths exaggerate and parables emphasize irony in ways that seldom occur in life. Despite these distortions, myths and parables ultimately draw their staying power from the truths they attempt to convey. The myths of Domingo Monterrosa are important to the young officers of the military corps and have received significant support from the official propaganda services of the Salvadoran armed forces. One clique of "reform officers" has identified itself as the "Domingo Monterrosa brigade." These officers advocated a war of impunity against the FMLN. They believed such a war to be holy, divinely ordered. They believed that God favors their cause. They still express these beliefs in songs, legends and myths about Domingo Monterrosa. Well after the peace accords were signed and the FMLN heavily invested in its program of demobilization, this "reform" group placed ads in newspapers.

The faith of the poor differs from that of the armed forces. Despite their present suffering, the poor believe in the justice of their struggle and that one day these sufferings will be vindicated. They believe in the ultimate power of the powerless. They tell their own stories about Domingo Monterrosa. Their use of the historical facts surrounding Monterrosa's death expresses these beliefs in a parable that presages future disruptions in power.

The truth of the Monterrosa parable remains to be seen. God may favor the poor in history, but the sad fact is that little evidence of this favor has been seen in El Salvador in recent years. The poor continue to struggle for some modicum of justice. Even after the signing of a peace agreement the oligarchy and military continue to rule the country with an iron hand, meting out their brand of justice through death squads and clandestine killings. If God's "year of favor for the poor" is imminent, the poor of El Salvador certainly deserve it. They are also waiting.

TALKING ABOUT "TERRORISM"
On the Salvadoran Military Radio Network

Radio Cuscatlan, the official Salvadoran armed forces radio network, presents news programs, music, documentaries, editorial commentaries and opportunities for its listeners to express their views in call-in talk shows. *Radio Cuscatlan* expresses the ethos of the Salvadoran armed forces in a way that is uninhibited by diplomatic decorum or concern for international political correctness. Understanding this ethos is vitally important. This ethos—and not optimistic, political prognostics from the United States department of state—will determine with what fidelity the Salvadoran armed forces embark on self-reform or respect their negotiated peace with the FMLN. What is more, the text of *Radio Cuscatlan's* daily programming is proof of how much the armed forces need to change beyond the reforms demanded by the peace accords.

The following analysis was made from broadcasts during the November 1989 FMLN offensive. At that time, COPREFA—the armed forces' press committee—was empowered by the high command to act as the government's official censor. WSAX, the archdiocesan radio station, chose to go off the air rather than submit to censorship and become, in effect, an organ of military propaganda. Many other radio stations followed the example of WSAX, and *Radio Cuscatlan* effectively became the government's official radio station, broadcasting without competition.

Radio Cuscatlan's call-in shows during the months of November and December 1989 aired particularly virulent attacks against alleged FMLN "terrorists" and "terrorist supporters" such as the Salvadoran Jesuit community and Archbishop Rivera Damas. The military claimed that *Radio Cuscatlan* was not responsible for the content of the conversations reported over the network. This is a fatuous claim, considering the heavy military censorship the whole country was under at the time.

What is more, the repeated structure of the call-in shows exhibited an intentionality. First, excited, breathless listeners called in to report alleged atrocities committed by the FMLN. These calls were then followed by supposed students and former students from the National University and the Jesuit University who reported on efforts by their professors to recruit them into the FMLN. In other instances callers denounced homilies or public positions of Archbishop Rivera Damas and Auxiliary Bishop Rosa Chavez and accused them of supporting the FMLN. Professors, priests and bishops were labeled "communists" and blamed for the atrocities previously reported. These accusations were followed by a rousing patriotic anthem, perhaps the "Ballad of (Colonel) Domingo Monterrosa," the national anthem of El Salvador, or other martial music. This sequence was then followed by a brief news report of the most recent (also alleged) victories of the armed forces against the "terrorist" insurgents.

Then the cycle was repeated: atrocities, reports of church and university collaboration with the "terrorists," anthems and news. If this pattern had been repeated only once or twice, one could accept the possibility of coincidence. But it was repeated for hours on end throughout the offensive and the weeks that followed. The very structure of *Radio Cuscatlan* programming was part of its content.

What did *Radio Cuscatlan* have to say to its listeners? It is ironic that Salvadorans probably hear more about communism on *Radio Cuscatlan* than on the FMLN's *Radio Venceremos*. The armed forces have identified the most diverse and unlikely group of candidates as communists. The list includes former United States ambassadors, members of the United States congress, former President Carter, Archbishops Romero and Rivera Damas, Bishop Gregorio Rosa Chavez, Lutheran Bishop Medardo Gomez, many priests and religious, reformist politicians and even former Salvadoran president Duarte, under whose administration the militarization of El Salvador escalated. To a certain extent the term is so inclusive it means nothing. More profoundly, communism refers to any effort to bring together poor peasants, workers and other disenfranchised people to improve their lot in life by changing the social and economic system. The military claims to support efforts of men and women to strive for individual betterment within the existing economic system. But any organized effort to change the system itself—even through peaceful means—it considers communism. This interpretation has had dire consequences for unions, for popular organizations and for the church, each of which seeks to effect change and pursues its respective missions through communities. They are frequently labeled communists by the armed forces.

For the producers of *Radio Cuscatlan* a terrorist is anyone who strives to achieve social change through armed struggle (a "communist" with a gun). For the armed forces and *Radio Cuscatlan*, "terrorist" does not refer to the indiscriminate use of violence to maintain the status quo. The word "terrorist" is only applied to the political left. This is significant because El Salvador has a terrorist law which many legal scholars claim could have been applied to the military killers of the Jesuits. But within El Salvador's government-military structure, violence is considered terror only when used by the left.

Radio Cuscatlan condemns terrorism and communism and extols fidelity to the fatherland. For the armed forces, "fatherland" embodies all that it means to be Salvadoran. It is a word which conjures images of home, family, rustic scenes of pastoral life under towering volcanoes. El Salvador's poor peasants are occupied with the task of survival. For them such images are surreal fantasies of the ruling class. Claiming as it does to represent all that El Salvador once was, should be and can be, the concept of fatherland is presented in contrast to anything foreign. According to *Radio Cuscatlan*, the unions, the church, the political parties on the left and especially the FMLN are based on "outside" ideas. The changes proposed by these "communists" are, according to *Radio Cuscatlan*, a "virus, a plague, an infection bringing misery to the Fatherland." The armed forces thus cite the values of the fatherland as their motivating force in waging war against their own people.

As noted above, the armed forces are not ostensibly opposed to efforts by individuals to achieve a better condition in life through their own efforts. *Radio Cuscatlan* frequently claims that the armed forces protect the freedom of Salvadorans who wish to work within the existing system to achieve a better life. But this freedom does not extend to efforts to change the system itself. The armed forces' mission to protect the country from outside intervention is identified over *Radio Cuscatlan* as synonymous with "rooting out terrorists" who agitate for such change.

Another "freedom" frequently extolled over *Radio Cuscatlan* is freedom of religion. Religious freedom is protected by El Salvador's constitution. To the Catholic, Lutheran, Episcopal and Immanuel Baptist churches' claims of persecution, *Radio Cuscatlan* has responded that there is freedom of religion in El Salvador. This assertion is true, as far as it goes. But it does not answer the charge that the churches are being persecuted. The armed forces have made it very clear that those churches which choose to participate in political activity and social activism cannot use the protection of the republic's freedom of religion as a protective cover. At the heart of this claim is the armed forces' insistence that religion should occupy itself solely with spiritual concerns. Within such strictures, clinics for the poor run by the churches are considered "political." The Catholic University is regarded as the "intellectual center for the terrorists." Christian base communities are labeled "communist cells." These labels are applied only to progressive churches. Fundamentalist sects such as Pat Robertson's 700 Club are frequently praised as authentic religions by *Radio Cuscatlan.*

For *Radio Cuscatlan* the function of language is often to confuse an issue rather than clarify it. This was very evident during the war in its use of two phrases, conflictive zone and air cover. The concept of conflictive zone was employed by the armed forces to restrict access of foreigners to parts of the country. As Archbishop Rivera Damas once noted, and as the FMLN proved in November of 1989, "all of El Salvador is a conflictive zone." By officially designating certain zones "conflictive" the armed forces could deny access to international observers and also limit the flow of medicines, food and building materials to persons displaced by the war. Within conflictive zones civilians were easily denied civil rights such as documentation, legal representation, *habeas corpus,* the freedom to travel and the right to assembly. More importantly, the Salvadoran air force disclaimed and continues to disclaim responsibility for any civilian deaths in the "conflictive zones." At times these included huge, heavily populated areas of the city of San Salvador and much of the countryside.

Air cover was a euphemism for bombing poor barrios, rural villages and refugee camps regarded as sources of "terrorist" support. *Radio Cuscatlan* frequently praised the Salvadoran air force for the "air cover" it provided ground troops during a military operation. The term implied that ground troops were in fact involved in the operation. Often this was not the case—the complete "kill quota" came from the air cover itself, predominantly from among the civilian population.

Civilian deaths were not denied by *Radio Cuscatlan.* In fact, two phrases heard over the network indicated the military's willingness to escalate the civilian death toll. These phrases were the solution of 1932 and the Guatemalan solution. These solutions to El Salvador's "terrorist problem" are still cited by the military as ominous threats against the Salvadoran population. In 1932 the Salvadoran dictator,

Maximillian Hernandez, ordered the slaughter of 30,000 peasants and Indians who had rebelled against his dictatorial rule. The poor refer to this as "The Great Killing of '32." The armed forces' radio holds up the great killing as a "solution" to the resistance of today's poor and workers against the rule of the oligarchy and military.

Radio Cuscatlan also cites the Guatemalan solution as a cure for El Salvador's ills. In the early 1980s Guatemala's armed forces undertook their own "Great Killing." Over four hundred villages in the mountainous northern provinces of Guatemala were dislocated as a result of military invasions and bombings. Many thousands were killed.

El Salvador's military regards the Guatemalan solution as a strategic option if the congress of the United States cuts military aid to El Salvador. The threat works, at least in the American press which shudders at the prospect of what will happen in El Salvador if no North American controls are in place. This follows ten years of allegedly training military officers in human rights and military discipline.

CONCLUSION

A people's speech provides insights into how they view the world and what values they uphold. The language one hears over *Radio Cuscatlan* says much about the values of the Salvadoran armed forces. Life is not valued, least of all the lives of the poor. Freedom is understood in extremely narrow terms. In English we would probably substitute the word "success" for where *Radio Cuscatlan* speaks of freedom. People are allowed to be successful, not free. (And many would contest this claim, with ample evidence.) Those who disagree with the conventional wisdom of the armed forces, as expressed by *Radio Cuscatlan,* are regarded as terrorists. Yet *Radio Cuscatlan* spreads its own kind of terror throughout El Salvador with its ominous references to the solution of 1932 and the Guatemalan solution.

Radio Cuscatlan is the official armed forces' broadcast network. In a country where the military has held ultimate authority over the government, including the judicial system, the opinions and news reported by *Radio Cuscatlan* are of interest to the whole population. It behooves those outside of El Salvador who support the Salvadoran military to pay close attention to its radio network. If the solutions which *Radio Cuscatlan* has proposed are enacted, there will be no excuse, no opportunity to declare, in stunned wonder, "We didn't know...how could we have imagined?"

Part Two:
FAITHFUL ENDURANCE

"Let him who has ears heed these words! For those destined for captivity, into captivity they go! For those destined to be slain by the sword, by the sword they will be slain! Such is the faithful endurance that distinguishes God's holy people."

Revelation 13:9-10

"The people united, will never be defeated" is a popular chant heard at union rallies, peace marches and assemblies of El Salvador's popular organizations. During the twelve year war, El Salvador's armed forces certainly curtailed the ability of El Salvador's poor and disenfranchised to organize, but they never stopped them. Now, after the peace accords, the process of organizing has escalated. Communities are still being born and forming networks with other communities. During the war, these networks were frequently detected; their leadership, decimated; members were killed, forced into exile or left with no option but to join the armed resistance. Still, the people persisted in re-forming communities and creating options for change that challenged the status quo.

"Part Two: Faithful Endurance" presents testimonies of women who opted for life in El Salvador. This meant an option for community-building and empowering the poor at great personal risk. As an FMLN combatant explained, "These women accepted the same risks as those of us incorporated into the armed struggle, but they did so without relying on weapons. They are the valiant ones." The valiant ones include nuns, community health workers, literacy teachers, community organizers and old story-tellers who kept alive the memory of suffering and the hopes of the people. During episodes of "low intensity warfare" in the province of San Salvador, directorate two of the

51

first infantry brigade, San Carlos battalion often identified the valiant ones as special targets. First, the air force or artillery units would "soften" the area under attack. Then the army moved in, often accompanied by units of the national guard. In the ensuing confusion, agents from the second directorate would seek out the valiant ones and execute them. In this way their deaths were not counted as executions (a human rights abuse) but as "casualties of war."

These chapters describe some of the work of the valiant ones who faithfully endured the struggle for liberation, even when abandoned by the church. To a North American reader, some of their efforts may appear rather innocuous. But any activity that built community, empowered the poor or challenged the status quo in El Salvador was regarded by the military as subversive and meriting the special attention of agencies like the Second Directorate.

These testimonies were all collected during the war and so reflect a relationship of the people to the FMLN that has changed significantly since the peace accords. It is important to point this out because references to FMLN activities reported in the present tense need to be understood as history. The FMLN is now a legitimate political force, not a guerrilla army.

THREE PORTRAITS OF THE SALVADORAN RESISTANCE

Laura Santiago grew up in the village of San Pedro, near the Guazapa volcano, in the country of El Salvador. Her peasant parents leased a small plot of land for growing beans and vegetables. They paid for this land with their labor. During the months of November and December Laura, her seven brothers, two sisters, mother and father harvested coffee for the landowner, not on Guazapa, but on the more-distant volcano of San Salvador. After they had picked enough coffee beans to lease their land, they earned an additional four hundred dollars. This they used to buy clothing, medicine, perhaps a few chickens and some small niceties for their one-room house.

In 1980, when Laura was seventeen years old, her family fled Guazapa and sought refuge in the capital of San Salvador. The incident that forced this exodus left an indelible scar on Laura's soul. Her parents were members of the Union of Salvadoran Peasants. In October 1980 the union asked the landowner for a raise in pay. The union leaders explained that because of rising prices workers could no longer afford basic necessities for their families. The landowner listened to the leaders but then informed them that wages depended on international prices. At least for that year, he said, there could be no raise. The union leaders responded that if the peasants did not receive a wage increase, the union would strike.

That night the Salvadoran national guard visited San Pedro. They led Laura's father and nine other men to a ditch next to the landowner's house. They killed the men, castrated them and stuffed their severed genitals into their mouths. The people found the corpses the next morning. Terrified, they buried their dead, packed their few belongings and began the long trek down the highway to the capital of San Salvador.

Laura met Juan Gonzalez while on this exodus. They became friends and eventually married. They found refuge in the camp established by the Catholic Church in the major seminary in San Salvador. Their child, Oscar Gonzalez Santiago, was born a year later. Oscar spent his first two years in that seminary. He first stepped outside on June 13, 1983 when Laura and Juan returned to Guazapa with thirty other families.

The families who resettled near Guazapa dug latrines, laid out roads, and, with the assistance of the church, secured a loan to purchase bricks, cement, wood and sheet metal. Men, women and children all worked together building their houses. When all thirty-one homes were completed they held a mass of thanksgiving. During this mass each family was assigned a home by lottery.

Once, when Oscar had fallen ill with dysentery in the refugee camp, Laura had gone to the camp infirmary for medicine. There she learned about a course for community health workers. After making some inquiries, Laura enrolled. Over the next year she completed two levels in the four-level program for community health workers. When Laura returned to Guazapa she formed a committee for community health. This committee taught the people about the microbes that infect water and cause dysentery, how to prepare water for drinking and how to rehydrate babies suffering from dysentery and diarrhea. Laura assumed responsibility for the clinic's small pharmacy and began a level-one course for her own committee. Once a month she took the bus into the capital to continue her own schooling.

As Laura's reputation as a health worker spread to other small villages on Guazapa the small clinic became over-burdened with patients. Laura asked a few of the women who came from these villages to volunteer some time to the clinic. She began a training program and soon had teams of health workers visiting the outlying villages teaching preventative health.

From May until August there is rain almost every night and then it is dry for the rest of the year. In the countryside drinking water comes from wells. The health workers explained to the people that their wells must be deepened and, in some cases, moved a safe distance uphill from latrines. They explained that animals must be kept in pens because the feces of animals pollutes the drinking water and animals that eat human feces become sick and infect humans. In many villages, the people refused to listen. It takes a great deal of effort to dig a new well and people did not relish this task. The health workers responded by explaining that clean water was the only solution to the horrible dysentery that killed so many children. In other villages the people listened and agreed. When the effects of these efforts became evident, other villages moved their wells.

Preventative health requires community action. If a village moves a well to high ground but one family continues to dispose of waste uphill from the well, the effort is wasted. The community health workers spend as much time developing decision-making strategies in the villages as talking about health. As Laura explained to her co-workers, these efforts were worthwhile. She pointed out to them, "It is easier to prevent dysentery than to cure it."

Laura's husband, Juan, found work as a laborer in the capital. He became a brick carrier earning three dollars a day. After deducting the cost of bus fare to and from work, Juan earned barely enough to buy food and clothes for his family. On May 1, 1985 Juan joined thousands of Salvadoran workers in a demonstration in San Salvador. While returning home, Juan and two companions were arrested by the national police. They were sent to a political prison and detained without trial. When Laura learned of her husband's detention she attempted to secure his release. But Laura was told that she had been misinformed. There was no Juan Gonzalez in custody and no record of his arrest. As Salvadorans put it, Juan "had been disappeared."

Laura returned home in despair.

She continued training community health workers. She was offered a small salary by the church and she enrolled Oscar in a church-sponsored day care center. Laura continued to hope that Juan would return to her, but this was a faint hope. She poured herself into her work. By 1986 Laura completed the fourth level of the training course and was supervising seven teams of health workers north of the capital.

Laura admits that at times she funneled medicines to the guerrillas on Guazapa. "That is my work," she says, "to get medicines to those who need them. The *muchachos* (guerrillas) also have sick and wounded." Laura never actually visited the guerrillas' camps. She passed the medicines to a young woman who came to the clinic twice a month. There were times when Laura could not spare supplies. "I had to decide," she said, "and sometimes I judged that the needs of the people in the villages were greater than those of the muchachos."

But something went wrong. The national guard detected the courier route supplying Guazapa and Laura's contact was arrested. Under torture she implicated Laura. Laura was arrested; she was raped and forced to eat her meals like a dog—refried beans served on a plate of human feces.

Even under torture Laura could not implicate others. She only knew the one courier. The police tried to get Laura to identify priests and nuns working in archdiocesan social programs as "terrorists." But she refused to do this. Five days after she had been arrested, quite unexpectedly Laura was released.

She returned home, anxious to find her little boy. He was safe and being cared for by the day-care teacher. Laura nearly smothered Oscar in her hugs and kisses. She says that Oscar was like a wiry monkey. He clung to her neck and wrapped his legs around Laura's waist, refusing to let go until that night when he fell asleep in his mother's arms.

At dawn on the morning after her release, Laura was awakened by a squad of national guardsmen. They questioned her about the "terrorists" posing as health promoters in the Guazapa region. Laura denied knowing anything about this. One of the soldiers slammed his rifle butt into Laura's face. She fell back onto her bed and that is when the soldiers discovered little Oscar.

Two soldiers took Oscar from his mother's bed and tugged at his arms and legs, as if to draw and quarter him. The captain continued to question Laura who continued to deny any knowledge of the guerrillas' movements around Guazapa. The soldiers then took Oscar outside. Laura heard one of them say "the fence" and she screamed.

By the time the soldiers escorted Laura outside, Oscar's two captors had him stretched over a barbed wire fence. Laura screamed. She promised to tell the national guard anything they wanted to know. She promised to work as an informer. But Laura's potential worth as an informer was finished.

The captain nodded to the two men holding Oscar. They dragged Oscar over the barbed wire. He screamed, called out for his mother and then, mercifully, he lost consciousness. The soldiers continued to drag Oscar over the wire until the flesh fell from his bones and his entrails became twisted in the coils. They did not ask Laura any more questions or hurt her further. What horror could match a mother's pain as she unraveled her son's viscera from the coils of a barbed wire fence?

Laura buried Oscar nearby. She packed her small medicine bag with penicillin and joined the guerrillas on Guazapa where she now works as a medic.

* * *

Not all FMLN supporters were from poor backgrounds. Not all were directly affected by the oppression and horrors of the war.

Carlota Lopez is a literacy teacher who works in the province of Morazan, in an area that remained under FMLN control throughout the war. Carlota grew up in a middle class family sympathetic to reform, but uninvolved in political life. Carlota was not converted to the FMLN by political rhetoric or by the horrors suffered by the faceless poor. Carlota joined the FMLN after she became friends with a poor woman who was arrested and "disappeared." Suddenly the poor were not faceless. When Carlota's friend was "disappeared," the veil that had separated Carlota from the poor dissolved and she crossed the line separating reform from revolution.

Carlota was raised in the capital of San Salvador. Her father, Pepe Lopez, had worked as an electrician in Guatemala and upon returning to El Salvador was hired by a firm that installs electrical wiring on government construction projects. Carlota's mother is a teacher in the government school system. With both parents working, Carlota grew up in comfortable circumstances. She shared her father's interest in electrical engineering and was intent on applying to the engineering school at the National University when she graduated from St. Dominic's High School in 1986.

The nuns who teach at St. Dominic's are members of the Dominican Order. Like many Catholic religious groups, the Dominicans made a "preferential option for the poor" after the Second Vatican Council. They continued to staff middle class high schools like St. Dominic's, but also assumed responsibility for three poor "relocation settlements" north of the city. They attempted to integrate both ministries by involving their middle-class high school students in various projects in these resettlements.

It was on such a project that Carlota first encountered El Salvador's poor. She volunteered to work one day a week with a community health worker at the clinic in Santo Tomas, a village north of the city. This health worker, Adela Casteneda, had been trained by Laura Gonzalez. Adela was intelligent but she could not read. This made her apprehensive about distributing medicines because the labels were undecipherable to her. At first Carlota helped Adela by simply reading labels to her. In the afternoon, when there were fewer patients to occupy them, Carlota taught Adela to read. She did this by creating word games that associated printed words with rhymes. Soon everything in the clinic had a small card attached with its name carefully printed in block letters.

Two months after Carlota started working at Santo Tomas, the clinic was visited by Laura Gonzalez. Carlota had heard about Laura, but was surprised by her youth. Laura spent the morning working with Carlota and Adela, watching carefully as the two women played their word game. That afternoon Laura asked Carlota where she had learned to teach. Carlota explained that her mother was a teacher and that these games were variations on learning rhymes her mother had taught her. Laura looked long and hard at Carlota. She thanked her for giving this "gift" to Adela. Her parting words were, "If you could teach more women to read in this easy manner, Salvador would achieve peace without war."

Previously, Carlota had not regarded reading as a "gift" nor associated the ability to read with peace. When she graduated from high school she still went to the National University, but she declared education as her major. Carlota's father was pleased. "Women should not be engineers," he said. "They are better as teachers."

Carlota's professor of education insisted that his students learn by immersion. He required that each student volunteer in a literacy program for which they would be evaluated and given credit. Carlota returned to Santo Tomas and asked Adela if her village would be interested in starting a literacy program. Adela was enthusiastic but said that she would have to bring the proposal to the community council. Other communities had experienced difficulties with the police when they introduced adult literacy programs. The next week Adela and the president of the community council visited Carlota at the National University and agreed to the project. It was also agreed that Adela would be Carlota's assistant.

Carlota traveled to Santo Tomas every Friday afternoon. Classes were held Friday evening. Due to the danger of traveling at night, Carlota stayed with Adela and returned home Saturday morning. The two women continued to work together, and as Adela became more involved in the class, her reading skills improved dramatically.

On April 3, 1987, Adela met Carlota at the university. The two women intended to visit a bookstore in downtown San Salvador and purchase books for their reading program. As they were leaving the university, the national police set up a cordon around the perimeter to check students' identification papers. Adela was detained because she was not a student and her identification indicated that she was from a zone known to be sympathetic to the FMLN.

Carlota insisted on accompanying her friend to the police headquarters. Carlota had never experienced trouble with the police and she was confident that her explanation would set things right. The police reluctantly agreed to let her accompany Adela and the two women soon found themselves sitting in a waiting room in the national police headquarters in downtown San Salvador.

The police captain in charge of the interrogation demanded Carlota's and Adela's papers. Both women produced their papers. While the captain was inspecting these, Adela motioned for Carlota to notice a sign hanging on the wall. "It says they can only hold us for seventy-two hours," she said.

The captain overheard this exchange. He returned Carlota's identification and told her to leave. When Carlota insisted on leaving with Adela, the captain replied, "We know that this woman is not who she claims to be."

"She is Adela Casteneda. I have known her for two years," Carlota said.

"She is not. Her papers clearly state that Adela Casteneda cannot read. I heard this woman read that sign to you."

Carlota tried to explain that she had taught Adela to read. The captain explained that if Adela was innocent, she would be freed. Carlota was forced to leave the police headquarters. Adela called out for Carlota to contact her family and the archdiocesan human rights office. The next day, Carlota returned with Adela's husband and a lawyer from the legal aid office of the archdiocese. "There is no record of an arrest of Adela Casteneda at the National University," Carlota was told. "In any event, she is not here now. Check her home later in the day. She probably spent the night with a boyfriend."

But Adela was not home. She "had been disappeared."

Carlota was visited by the police two days following Adela's disappearance. The police warned Carlota that she should no longer travel north of the capital. "There has been too much trouble up there and we are afraid that the terrorists might kidnap you." They also asked about the literacy program in Adela's village. It was evident from their questions that they had gotten some information from Adela before her friend "had been disappeared."

Carlota did not finish the term at the university. She heeded the police and did not return to Adela's village. Instead she went to Morazan and joined the FMLN civilian administration as a literacy teacher. Carlota still teaches in villages under FMLN control. "Adela Casteneda was my friend," she says. "Although we only knew each other for two years and came from different backgrounds, we loved each other like sisters. Something I learned as a child was that you cannot stand idly by when a friend suffers. I joined the revolution in El Salvador because no other route was left to me to seek justice for

Adela's death." Carlota begins every new class by telling her students the story of Adela Casteneda, warning them: "Reading can be danger-ous—thinking is more dangerous still."

* * *

For much of the war, Vicki Vasquez worked within the FMLN as a community organizer. She is now a political organizer. Ironically, her decision to join the FMLN was made by the armed forces of El Salvador.

Vicki was born in 1965, the oldest of four children of Felix and Mercedes Vasquez. Vicki's family is from the province of Chalatenango. Her parents were small landowners. They farmed twen-ty acres in the area of the Sumpul River near the Salvadoran-Honduran border.

Vicki's father was a catechist. Every Saturday and Sunday he trav-eled from one village to another along the Sumpul River reading the scriptures to the people and leading them in prayer and an analysis of the Salvadoran reality. Vicki first accompanied her father on his cate-chetical rounds when she was seven years old. Vicki enjoyed the free-dom from household chores afforded by these expeditions. What she liked best, however, was basking in the esteem that the Sumpul River people held for her father. At home he was just a hard-working farmer. Along the Sumpul he was a man of some importance.

The Salvadoran armed forces' invasions of Chalatenango increased in frequency and brutality between 1977 and 1980. On March 24, 1980 the people of Chalatenango received word that Archbishop Oscar Romero had been killed. Two weeks later the Salvadoran armed forces received a huge increase in military aid from the United States and began an offensive against Chalatenango. Vicki and her father were in the village of La Arada at seven in the morning when the army arrived on May 14, 1980. The army simply came into town and started tossing grenades into the houses.

"We were in the plaza preparing to return home. My father and I looked down the main street of La Arada and saw a soldier toss a baby into the air while his companions shot at it. They were not very good marksmen. It took three tosses before one of them hit the baby. It exploded, raining soft flesh and blood over the soldiers. The sol-diers seemed to enjoy it.

"At first we did not move. We felt as if we were under a spell.

Then my father grabbed me and we ran down the street away from the soldiers."

Vicki and her father joined the people of La Arada in their flight to the Sumpul River. As they began the descent to the river, they were attacked by two helicopters. The smaller group that included Vicki and her father fled across the mountainside and entered a deep, vine-covered ravine.

"I will never forget the two hours we spent in that ravine," Vicki says. "There were perhaps thirty of us lying on the ground. We could see through the vines to the edge of the chasm where the soldiers were probing and poking their rifles, looking for some sign of where we had fled. There was a woman with two children near me. I recognized her from our previous visits to La Arada. Whenever she spoke in our Bible classes she talked about her children. She did this regardless of what we were discussing. She spoke of them as examples of God's love. This woman's children gave her ideas about Mary's relationship to Jesus, and Jesus' relationship to his apostles. For her, these children were life itself.

"Her three year old was frightened but she understood the need to be quiet. The baby was tired and hungry. The soldiers heard her when she cried and returned to search the edge of the ravine. This woman took a piece of cloth, rolled it into a ball and stuffed it in her baby's mouth. When the baby lost consciousness, the mother removed the cloth. But the baby regained consciousness and cried out louder. I will never forget the look of horror on that mother's face as she replaced the cloth into her baby's mouth and held her as the infant suffocated."

When the people of La Arada thought that the soldiers had departed, they sent two men to see if it was safe to continue. When these men returned, they reported that the soldiers had left. The people were afraid to return to their homes and they decided to cross the Sumpul River into Honduras.

They crawled out of the ravine. The mother who had killed her daughter held the tiny corpse as if clinging to the hope that her baby was still alive. They walked to the river, gradually joining other bands of refugees fleeing the armed forces. By the time they reached the river they numbered well over six hundred.

The scene at the shoreline was one of bedlam. Things became worse when somebody cried out that the army was preparing to descend on the river. Vicki's father called out to her, "Grab hold of one of the young ones, and get into the river." Vicki took the hand of the three year old girl whose sister had died in the ravine and waded into the river. Her father took two young children by their hands and followed. As the river filled with refugees it became difficult to see the Honduran shore.

Vicki is not sure who started the shooting, the Honduran or Salvadoran army. The bullets seemed to come from both river banks. She glanced back at her father and saw a bullet hit his head. He quickly sank beneath the river's surface. The two children he was helping were swept away by the current and drowned.

As Vicki approached the shore she heard the soldiers shouting that Salvadorans could not cross into Honduran territory. Vicki held the little girl close and let the current pull her down river. She worked with the current to move closer to the Honduran shore. This decision probably saved Vicki's life.

Down river there were fewer soldiers. As she neared the shore, Vicki became entangled in some fish nets. That evening a Honduran fisherman rescued her. The little girl she had carried was dead—two bullets had entered her chest. Vicki did not even notice this until the fisherman took her ashore. Six hundred men, women and children were massacred at the Sumpul River. For days the bodies that littered both shores provided a carrion feast for vultures and dogs. Vicki had no idea how extensive the slaughter had been. She did not know if her village had also come under attack or if her mother, sister and brothers were safe. Vicki considered returning home but decided instead to go to a refugee camp in Honduras.

Vicki joined a catechetical team and began forming Christian base communities in the camp at Mesa Grande. These communities met weekly to reflect on the word of God and to analyze their plight in light of the scriptures. Vicki enjoyed her work but was unhappy at the camp. She felt worse when she attended religious services of any kind. Vicki couldn't understand this. She had worked with her father as a catechist. She had admired Archbishop Romero and found encouragement in the church's preferential option for the poor. Yet the masses, prayer services and other religious events at Mesa Grande only depressed her.

On November 4, 1984, Vicki was asked to lead a discussion around Psalm 137. She read the text:

> By the streams of Babylon
> we sat and wept
> when we remembered Zion.

On the aspens of that land
 we hung up our harps,
Though there our captors asked of us
 the lyrics of our songs,
And our despoilers urged us to be joyous:
 "Sing for us the songs of Zion!"
But how could we sing a song of the Lord
 in a foreign land?
If I forget you, Jerusalem,
 may my right hand be forgotten!
May my tongue cleave to my palate
If I place not Jerusalem
 ahead of my joy.

When she had finished reading this text, one of the people exclaimed, "I know what this means. This is how we all feel. How can we sing our Salvadoran songs in this foreign land?"

Vicki then understood why religious services at Mesa Grande had made her so unhappy. She associated the songs with her own land, but singing them only aggravated her homesickness and concerns for her family. Two days later Vicki left the camp in the company of a young guerrilla. Today she works with the FMLN in Chalatenango as a community organizer. She has no identification papers. She is still afraid that she will be one day identified, arrested and killed.

Vicki no longer calls herself a catechist. She regards her community organizing in the "liberated territories" as the "work of the gospel" but she distinguishes it from catechetical work. "We Salvadorans regard the gospel as incarnated in history," Vicki says. "But its incarnation is not the gospel. I have chosen to work on El Salvador's historical project because of my religious convictions."

CONCLUSION

These women's lives help to interpret the reality of El Salvador's struggle and shed light on why young men and women, old peasants, the middle class and the poor continue to support the FMLN.

Initially, Laura chose to become a community health worker. But she chose to do this in a country where health workers are persecuted. The Salvadoran government, military and oligarchy object to the organizing that takes place around efforts to prevent sickness.

Health workers in El Salvador stress prevention over cure. There are not enough medicines and doctors to treat people. To organize for better health, people must cooperate. Community organization, decision-making processes, consensus building, accountability: these are the foundation of preventative medicine. Laura understood that when people organize themselves for health, they will discuss other things as well—things such as the relationship of health to working conditions, the lack of funds to purchase medicines and the possibility of buying more and better foods in cooperative arrangements. These issues are not strictly health issues, but they touch on health. In El Salvador, they are still considered subversive by those in power.

These women were not recruited to join the FMLN by Cubans or Russians. Nor were they motivated by Marxist polemics. When forced to choose between hope and despair, they chose hope and they would so choose again. Although peace has been declared, six months after the signing none of these women have contacted old friends and family. They lived through most of the war in danger because, in El Salvador, hope had dangerous consequences. According to them, it still does.

Laura, Carlota and Vicki joined the FMLN because other options for change had become closed to them. The conditions that led Laura, Carlota and Vicki to opt for the FMLN have not changed. Their lives, and the lives of many others, remain in danger until a civilian-controlled police force with participation of the FMLN is deployed throughout El Salvador. Until that happens, American increases in aid for the police threaten these women's lives. The irony is that during the war, American support for the Salvadoran military-controlled security forces encouraged the military and police to be more abusive. As a result, more men and women joined the FMLN. Now, in post-war El Salvador, continued abuses of human rights by the police motivate many young people—supporters of the FMLN—to register for the new, civilian-controlled police academy.

An earlier version of this chapter was published in The Clinton Street Quarterly, *Vol. 12, No. 1, Spring, '90.*

THE *GUINDA*

When she was twelve years old, Juanita Martinez was forced to watch as the Salvadoran national guard rounded up the men in her village of Santa Lucia, bound them in groups of five or six, doused them with kerosene and set them on fire. La matanza, *or "The Great Killing," of 1932 was the Salvadoran military's response to the effort of the peasants to secure their rights, first through political organizing and, when that failed, through armed rebellion. Since 1932 the Great Killing has been impressed on the consciousness of every Salvadoran.*

But memories fade and ten years ago our young people again began to dream of freedom. I had no such dreams. I saw my father burn alive. My mother held me in her arms as we watched the burning flesh fall off the bones of my brothers. After seeing such things, who could dream of freedom? No, for me the cost was too high! But these young people—they don't realize. Or else they have more courage than we had. We'll see.

I can't say exactly when our recent troubles began. It seems that we've always lived with difficulties. I'll start my testimony in mid-November 1978. That's when we went up to the large plantations to pick the coffee. The landowners had sent word throughout the countryside that the season would begin on November 14. The landowners were nervous. The rains had come late in May, delaying the maturing of the coffee beans. Tradition held that the harvest end by December 24. The landowners knew that it would be difficult to get us back onto their plantations after Christmas and they feared losing some of the crop.

We rose at 3:30 in the morning on November 14—old people, children, men and women—and began the long trek up the volcano of Chinchontepec. We arrived at the plantation at around six o'clock in the morning and registered with the foremen. A man from the police checked our identification papers against a list. Those whose names appeared on that list were taken away by the national guard. In 1978 three men from Santa Lucia were arrested at harvest time. We never learned what became of them.

You'll find some old fools in this country who'll tell you about the happy days of the coffee harvest. I think maybe age, pain or suffering has dulled their wits. There was nothing happy about the harvest except that we were guaranteed work for two months and on December 24 we had some money to buy a few gifts, maybe a toy for the little one in the family or some turkey for the Christmas tamales.

Who could be happy working under such conditions? If we accidently broke one branch of a coffee tree we were fined a day's wage. If we broke two branches in a single season, we were fired. The foremen even counted the beans under the trees where families worked. We were paid by the basket and for every bean lost the wage for one basket was deducted from our pay.

My grandson, Elias, had gone with me on every harvest since his mother died when he was four; 1978 was his fifteenth harvest. Every year since he was old enough to think for himself, he had asked me: "Grandmother, why do we let them cheat us like this?"

"Be quiet," I would answer. "Who gave you permission to ask questions?"

"Why do we need permission to ask questions?" he persisted. "If we need permission to ask questions we're no better than slaves."

"We're alive," I told him. "And if you keep this up, more than just you and I will suffer. In 1932 they didn't just kill my brother—who asked these same questions—they killed all of our men."

"These are new times," my grandson said. "We can't live in the shadow of 1932 forever."

My grandson had no difficulty finding others who thought as he did. They formed a group and walked together during the long trek up the volcano and in the evening when they returned home. We old folks were too tired to talk. But when these young people walked, they talked and talked and talked.

The harvest ended on December 23 and we collected our small wages. I remember my anger when the foreman told me that he'd deducted the value of fifteen baskets of beans from my pay. "We counted many more lost beans under your trees, Doña Juanita, but only deducted the value of these fifteen baskets because of your past service to the landowner. Next year you must be more careful."

The hardest part was appearing grateful for their thievery. My God! We'd begun work an hour earlier and continued until dark to finish this harvest before Christmas. Fifteen baskets was three days' work. Three hard days of work without pay because of a few lost coffee beans that wouldn't fill a cup!

On December 24 I forgot my anger. I prepared a wonderful meal of beans, rice cooked with turkey, tamales and coffee. We ate, my grandson and I, until we could eat no more. Then we rested and ate some more. When we finished eating, I gave my grandson his gift—a pair of leather shoes so that he could return to school in January. He was angry I had spent so much money on his present and threatened to return the shoes to the market. Then he thanked me.

My grandson gave me his gift. I suppose it is a small thing to you, but I was so happy that I couldn't speak. You see, my grandson didn't collect a wage for his work. We worked together and shared the same wage. I couldn't imagine where he had gotten the money to buy this gift. He explained that he and some friends had returned to the plantation every Sunday to pick coffee. With this little extra—after six weeks of Sundays—my grandson had earned enough to buy me a bottle of shampoo. I still have the bottle although I used the last of the shampoo last Easter.

ORGANIZING

In the late 1970s, peasants who worked as seasonal laborers on El Salvador's large coffee plantations began to organize. The Chinchontepec volcano in the province of La Paz was one of the first areas where workers went on strike for higher wages.

My grandson was one of the organizers of the 1979 strike. One of the young men who worked alongside my grandson was Antonio Moran, a seminarian from San Salvador. Antonio was granted permission every year to work with his mother during the coffee harvest. Another of the key organizers in Santa Lucia was a young woman I had known since she was born, Corelia Casteñeda. Corelia was different. She had an education. Ten years earlier her mother's sister had left for the United States and had sent money to pay for Corelia's schooling. I think she may even have completed high school, although I'm not sure.

These young people frequently met in my kitchen so I heard most of what they said. At first I was glad to see Elias spending so much time with Antonio and Corelia. But after their first few meetings I knew we were in for trouble in Santa Lucia, and that Antonio, Corelia and my grandson were going to be in the middle of it.

Of all the young people who helped organize the workers, Antonio was the most insistent. This came as no surprise because this has been our experience with priests and future priests. He would preface his opinions with "Monseñor says." "Monseñor" was a reference to the new archbishop of San Salvador, Oscar Romero. I have to confess I, too, listened to his homilies on the radio every Sunday morning even though I had long ago stopped going to church. Having heard Monseñor's homilies, I was frightened to think what Antonio and the others were planning.

"It's our right," my own boy exclaimed on a number of occasions.

"It's not a question of rights or what Monseñor says," Corelia added. "The truth is that we learned something this year. They need us. For ten months of the year we are less than the dirt under their feet. But in November and December, they need us. Everything that this country produces for export—coffee, sugar, cotton—must be harvested in these months. It is during this time and only then that we have power. We have them by the balls and all we have to do is squeeze."

At one of their meetings, Corelia said to me: "Doña Juanita, Elias has told us how your family were once labor organizers and how you lived through the Great Killing of 1932. You have some experience. What do you think we should do? How should we organize?"

I knew that I was being flattered into helping these young people. I hesitated but then answered: "Back in 1932 we had no way to communicate with the city," I said. "Today I can go down to Pedro's store and use his phone to call the capital. One reason our struggle failed in '32 was because we peasants had no way to communicate with the workers in the city. Also we now have television. If we had had television in '32 who can imagine the world standing by as 30,000 of our people were horribly killed . . ."

"So what you're telling us, Doña Juanita, is that we need to coordinate with the popular organizations in the capital and to have press coverage." This was a statement and not a question. I didn't even know what "press coverage" meant. I assumed the worst.

The following months were busy ones. My grandson returned to school and completed fifth grade. Monseñor Romero visited our little church and even I went to the mass that he celebrated. I don't like priests and I like bishops even less. Still, even I loved this man. After mass, Monseñor's assistant kept whispering in his ear and pulling him toward the car. But Monseñor insisted that our young people show him Santa Lucia before he left us. We all walked with him. And when he came to the place where six weeks earlier the *guardia* had killed four peasants, he stopped to pray. During this prayer I had a horrible feeling in my stomach. It wasn't because of what Monseñor said, but because what he said was true. "This killing was wrong," Monseñor said. "And we will suffer these wrongs no more."

LAND TO THE PEOPLE

In October 1979, just before the coffee harvest was to begin, a group that called itself the Federation of Salvadoran Peasants–Union of Farmworkers announced that the peasants were demanding a raise in the rate of pay for every basket of coffee. This was true in the province of La Paz, and in other provinces as well. The 1979 harvest was to begin early, on November 4.

My grandson and his friends formed "The November 4 Committee of Santa Lucia." I became their "advisor." "The November 4 Committee" met in my house the night before the harvest was to begin. Antonio was back from the capital. Other friends of my grandson had joined the committee as well as my niece, Ana Maria. There were also a few new faces that night. From the strange way they talked I assumed these newcomers were from the city. I didn't understand much of what they said. But I did realize when they talked about "the masses" they meant us, the peasants. When they talked about the "oligarchy" they meant more than the fourteen families who own so much of the land in El Salvador. They meant all the rich. I remember that when Jose Humberto asked who would pay for the extra wages we were demanding, the answer was "the imperialists." That meant you North Americans.

"The November 4 Committee" talked well into the morning, and I was quite sure that, if we did start work the next day, these young people would pick very little coffee. When the meeting ended I insisted everybody stay the night. In El Salvador it is dangerous to be out at night. The *guardia* needs only the slightest pretext to kill.

Our first confrontation was quite short and peaceful. All of the peasants—those from Santa Lucia as well as those from the surrounding villages—refused to enter the plantation until the landowner met with us. At first the foreman refused to send our message to the hacienda. But when he did, the landowner replied that he would only meet with our leaders. We said we had no leaders; we only had spokesmen. Anything we had to say could be said in front of all the people, as we were united in our demands. The foreman left to inform the landowner of this development and returned with a promise: "The *patron* knows this strike was not your idea but that of communist agitators from the city. He promises to forget everything that has happened here if you begin registering for work."

In response, we started chanting, "Forty cents a basket. Daily pay." This was the wage we were demanding (at the time, about ten U.S. cents) and also that we be paid at the end of every day. We knew their tricks. If we waited until December 23 to be paid the landowner would deduct our small gains from our pay.

The *guardia* was present but they made no effort to stop us. How could they? There were two thousand of us and only a handful of them. We were united. Their tactic had always been to take away our leaders. That morning, if they had attacked, we would have stopped them.

We stayed throughout the morning chanting and singing. "The people united, will never be defeated," was one chant. Another was "Enough now, enough now, land to the people." And there were more.

Our spokesmen, my grandson and the other members of "The November 4 Committee" stayed well-hidden in the midst of the crowd to protect their identities. I was toward the front. I must tell you that, although I was afraid and not at all sure we were doing the right thing, I was proud of my grandson.

Most of us left at mid-day. If we were not going to pick coffee, we had other work in the home. But every morning we returned to the plantation and presented our demands to the foreman. We shouted our chants and sang our songs.

On the last day of the week the landowner came down to talk with us. He was angry but I could also see that he was scared. Coffee must be harvested while ripe and on the tree. During these two months of the harvest the landowners are vulnerable. After one week of our strike, the over-ripe beans were already falling from the trees. A two month strike would have ruined the harvest. But, sadly, he had nothing to offer us. He refused to listen to us and simply repeated his earlier demand that we start work. The next day, we had our first trouble.

Other large plantations had been targeted and hundreds of

thousands of peasants across El Salvador had been striking at the same time. We asked the students from the National University to help us keep other communities informed of our efforts and to keep us informed of what was occurring in other parts of the country. Three of these students drove to Chalatenango on Friday afternoon to learn what they could of the strike in that part of the country. On Saturday night we received news that they'd been stopped by the *guardia*, pulled from their car and killed with machetes. They were buried in a common grave in Santa Lucia's cemetery.

On Sunday evening the landowner left in a truck piled high with his family's personal belongings. He was accompanied by the *guardia* and the gate to the plantation was left open. I have suffered much in my life, and especially in the past ten years. But the feeling of victory we shared on Monday morning when we entered the plantation gave meaning to all that suffering.

We didn't know what to make of the landowner and the *guardia* leaving. For most of Monday morning we walked around the part of the hacienda that had previously been off-limits to us. We saw many wonderful things and some strange things as well: there was a fountain with bubbling water inside the house; a large barn filled with old cars; another shed held an emergency electrical plant. There was a small barracks for the *guardia*, and there was a large cold room filled with sides of beef. Also in this room were coats made from animal fur. Some were dark, others were a beautiful silver color. We couldn't imagine at first why the landowner needed coats made of fur. Then my grandson said: "These coats are for the servants who work in this cold room preparing this meat." As I told you, Elias finished five years of school and was quite smart.

We looked at everything but took nothing except a side of beef for a barbecue.

We began working at eleven in the morning and we worked until dark. We had been completely taken by surprise by the departure of the landowner and the *guardia*. "Land to the people" had been a slogan for us, not a hope. So that night, after we finished eating, we sat down to talk and plan.

As was becoming the custom, the university students spoke first. "The land belongs to the people and the factories to the workers. We should harvest the coffee and share its profits equally." From what I had seen of the student who said this, I guessed that she had never picked a coffee bean in her life.

Other voices, less educated but perhaps more experienced, prevailed. Antonio spoke: "Monseñor says workers deserve a just wage and the landowners have a right to their property."

My grandson also spoke and it was his suggestion that we accepted. "We should harvest the coffee, prepare it for sale and share equally in the just wage of forty cents per basket. We should share this wage with those who stay behind to cook for us and to care for the small children. After deducting our wages and expenses we should return the profits to the landowner. We must prove that he can pay us a just wage and still make a profit—without the *guardia* standing over us."

So we worked. We worked harder than we'd ever worked before. Those of us from the outlying villages moved onto the plantation to start work earlier. In the evenings, after a meal of beans, rice and tortillas, we planned future projects. Even I began to hope. We discussed digging a six kilometer irrigation canal. We planned the fruit harvest and raising cattle.

I will die knowing what heaven is like. It is long days of hard work with the satisfaction of enjoying the fruits of your labor. We enjoyed heaven on Chinchontepec for ten days. We had our problems too, but we had the freedom to search for solutions. We had differences of opinion, especially with the young people from the university. But we knew that with time they would learn as much from us as we had from them.

It was only ten days but in that short time we started a school and dreamed of the day when our children would be able to read and write.

It was only ten days but we began work on that irrigation canal.

It was only ten days but we began a community health program and dreamed of the day when our children would not die at an early age from measles, malaria and dysentery.

Then, after ten days, the guardia returned and our *guinda* began.

THE FLIGHT

A guinda is a flight, often of thousands of people driven by fear. During the late 1970s and early 1980s the Salvadoran armed forces were completely indiscriminate in their bombardment and invasions of areas they deemed under guerrilla control. When the army arrived, the people fled, taking nothing but the clothes on their backs. Their flight was haphazard. Some people fled to the Honduran border. Others sought the protection of the church in San Salvador. The flights often lasted several days during which time

many people died, either from attacks by the military, starvation, thirst, expo-
sure or disease.

The plantation was on the northern side of Chinchontepec.
Many small villages were located on the skirt of the volcano. Those of
us who had moved onto Chinchontepec heard the first shots fired
from the helicopters as the *guardia* circled the villages of San Pablo
and Flores de Mayo below us. We could plainly see how, when the
people tried to flee these villages, they were shot down by the helicopters. But at first, the *guardia* stayed outside of the towns.

They were waiting for the tanks. When the tanks started firing,
those of us on Chinchontepec could hear them. Soon the sky over San
Pablo and Flores de Mayo was covered by a blanket of smoke. Then—it
was minutes after the slaughter had begun—someone screamed "The
guardia" and we rose like a huge wave. Two thousand of us from
seven towns began this *guinda*. Eighty survived.

We fled toward the village of Santa Rosa that straddled the
northern border of the plantation on the volcano's peak. Perhaps we
expected to find protection among its adobe walls. We pushed our
way up the volcano through terrain we knew well, calling out the
names of our friends and family.

As the helicopters finished their work below us, the sky began to
clear and we could see the destruction of San Pablo and Flores de
Mayo. The soldiers were now passing through these villages and set-
ting fire to the roofs of the standing houses. We saw mothers trying to
flee with their babies bundled in her arms. We saw them shot down
from the circling helicopters.

Our path went up the side of the volcano and soon joined another that crossed its summit. Santa Rosa was to the right. The path to
the left led to another plantation on the other side of Chinchontepec.
The *guardia* had set up two machine guns at this crossing. They
opened fire as the first of our people came within their sights. I had
stopped to search for my grandson and because of this delay I was
spared. I was not, however, spared the sight of my friends and neighbors cut down like corn stalks under a machete. Others, particularly
the children, seemed to explode when the bullets hit them.

Behind us the helicopters had finished their work and were now
advancing toward the plantation. We knew that if we stopped we'd
surely be killed, either by these helicopters or by the machine guns in
front of us. So we fled around the machine guns as they continued to
fire into us. How many died there, I do not know. I ran and fell, ran

and fell in the slippery, thick blood mixed with the dust of the volcano. I climbed over the bodies of friends and found myself stepping
on their faces in my flight to safety.

I was in the group that fled along the mountain path to Santa
Rosa. I was among the lucky ones because none of those who took the
road to the other side of the mountain survived. There were thirty of
us in the first group to enter Santa Rosa. We stared straight ahead,
refusing to look at the terrible sights around us. As we entered the
plaza, however, we could ignore the death and destruction no longer.
Santa Rosa is quite small but its plaza is one of the most beautiful in
the province of La Paz. In the very center of this plaza is a huge
mango tree. The people of Santa Rosa claimed that it had grown there
from before the time of the Spanish. Now, dangling from this tree
were over fifty bodies. Some hung from their necks while others had
been hung from their feet.

We stopped and stared. Then I cried out, for there among the
dead was Antonio, Santa Lucia's future-priest and Monseñor
Romero's voice in our short-lived struggle. As more people entered
the plaza we continued to stare in silence at the destruction. Burned
bodies lay in the paths around the plaza. We guessed from the way the
skirts were pulled up around the women's waists and the bruises on
their bodies that they had been raped—some apparently countless
times. And what they had done to the children of Santa Rosa! The
wall surrounding the church was lined with their severed heads. I realized then that we had not escaped the *guardia*; they had let us escape
to tell others of the power of their hate.

People continued to flow into the plaza. We now numbered over
two hundred, silently standing around that ancient mango tree. Then
I heard a voice call out above the crowd, "Antonio. Antonio. My God,
no. Antonio." It was a cry of desperation but it lifted my spirits
because it was the voice of my grandson.

"Elias," I cried.

"Grandmother. Is that you?" he answered. Others then started to
call out the names of their family and friends and the plaza soon
became a confusion of crying and the calling of names.

I found my boy and we embraced. I didn't want to release him
but finally he held me at arm's length and cried, "Mama, Corelia was
with Antonio last night. They came up to Santa Rosa to talk to the
people about starting a school. We've got to find her."

I helped my boy to search for his friend. First we searched the
streets along the sides of the plaza. Then we entered the church.

Apparently, the people had fled into the church thinking that God would somehow protect them. But God had offered no such protection. The front doors had been blown off their hinges by a weapon of great destruction. The bodies of men, women and children lay haphazardly across benches and in the aisles. None had been left alive and the mutilation was terrible.

In the sanctuary we saw the corpse of the only dead soldier. The knife that had killed him was still stuck in his stomach. Laying not five feet from him was our friend Corelia. Her hand—I assume it was the hand that had held the knife—had been cut off and lay a few feet above her head. She too had been raped repeatedly and was lying in a pool of blood still flowing from the stump of her hand.

My grandson fell onto Corelia, crying. I lifted him, as best I could. Others from our *guinda* were now entering the church via the main entrance. Some friends helped me to bring my boy back to the plaza where the people were now cutting down the bodies hanging from the mango tree.

We then planned the rest of our *guinda*. We decided to leave Santa Rosa by five separate routes. We felt that this would ensure that some of us would reach safety to tell what had happened. My grandson and I gathered about us as many people from Santa Lucia as we could find—about sixty in all—and began the trek down the southern side of Chinchontepec.

That first night we slept in a mango grove. The next morning, still without food or water, we continued down the mountainside. At mid-morning we were spotted by a small plane. The children began to cry. The men hesitated and became even more worried. One of them suggested "waiting for the helicopters to take us to safety"—as if the *guardia* had ever been our protectors! It was the women who kept the *guinda* moving forward.

I took charge of a young mother and her four children. The mother—Isabel was her name—was completely dazed and incapable of providing her small family with any leadership. Isabel took her nursing infant and I herded the three oldest in front of me. After another half hour we heard the thunder of approaching helicopters. We moved closer to the mountainside and hid under a ledge covered with vines and bushes.

The air became still. We huddled close together, waiting for death.

Isabel started to whimper. I scolded her, "Shhh.... Be strong. Be strong for your little ones."

Then the *guardia* came. At first we only heard their voices. When the sun moved higher in the sky, we could see them on the path below us. The first group passed without showing much interest in searching.

Then Isabel's baby started to cry.

"Feed her," I whispered.

"I've tried," she said, "but I have no milk."

"Put your little finger in her mouth."

"I did. She only cries more."

"Shhhh," I said. "The *guardia* is returning."

There was not much light under the brush but there was enough to see as Isabel placed her hand over her baby's mouth to smother its cries. I saw the baby turn red and then purple. I saw the tears form in Isabel's eyes as she glanced desperately down the mountainside waiting for the soldiers to leave. But they didn't leave; they lingered.

Isabel's face turned into a horrible mask of self-loathing as she suffocated her baby. She sacrificed this young one so that the rest of us could live. I've thought of Isabel and her baby often in the years since that *guinda*. The memory of her sacrifice has helped me to continue to hope and to struggle.

My grandson is in the mountains now, fighting with the guerrillas. I live here and I take every chance I can to tell people what happened on our *guinda* and to remind my people of what could have been if we'd had more than just ten days.

This testimony was recorded in June and July 1989. Doña Juanita Martinez died on November 18, 1989 when a rocket fired from an A-37 Dragonfly aircraft destroyed her home. Also killed were her niece, Ana Maria, and her grandson, Elias Juan Martinez, who was seeking refuge with his grandmother in the wake of the FMLN retreat from San Salvador.

PASTORAL WORK AS REBELLION

The young people from the village of Santa Lucia spend a great deal of time in front of the convent of the Passionist Sisters. Sometimes they just sit and talk with one another. I have often seen them doing their homework there, books perched on their knees, seated on the tree stumps and split logs scattered in front of the convent. Whenever they become discouraged—a perennial condition for the vast majority of El Salvador's young—Juanita Martinez or another member of the pastoral team helps them see the hidden possibilities of life. During the war, when friends or family members were killed, either in the war or by accident—or worse, when they were "disappeared"—pastoral workers like Juanita Martinez kept hope alive. She and her co-workers believe in the kingdom of God but at the same time they are participating in El Salvador's historical project to build a society of justice and equality.

The pastoral team at Santa Lucia does not devote all its attention to the young. They devote themselves to the many poor who visit the church. I do not think people visit the church primarily for financial support or consoling words. They visit because of the atmosphere created by the pastoral team. It is both affirming and challenging. Juanita Martinez's genius lies in the way she silently affirms and adeptly trains her co-workers to do the same. She challenges people to give more of themselves. She leads the destitute to their own hidden springs of strength.

El Salvador's military, oligarchy and other powerful institutions still regard Juanita and her co-workers as rebels, and with reason; they are part of the Christian tradition of prophetic rebellion. This chapter demonstrates how, in certain social circumstances, the casual association of youth in front of a church could be considered rebellious, and why, in the historical context of El Salvador's war and current social-political reality, a government would regard nuns, priests, catechists, health workers and literacy teachers as subversives.

77

THE PASTORAL OF LIBERATION

To be fully understood as an act of rebellion, the pastoral work at Santa Lucia needs to be situated within the specific historical context of El Salvador's history. The relationship of El Salvador's poor and working class to the oligarchy and military was defined in *la matanza*, or "The Great Killing" of 1932 in which 30,000 Indians and urban poor were massacred. After the great massacre the oligarchy defined itself as the "producers" and the Indians and other poor as "non-producers," that is, as "users" of national resources. The oligarchy maintained that it was their capital and not the labor of the Indians that allowed the plantations to produce crops for export. The government of El Salvador reflected this understanding in all national programs. The racism and classism inherent in this world-view was accepted and blessed by the Catholic Church.

Unrest continued after *la matanza* and galvanized in the decades of the 1970s and 1980s. The current wave of resistance has its roots in the Second Vatican Council's "opening to the world." In Latin America such openness implies listening to the poor. The Latin American bishops' conferences at Medellín and Puebla affirmed the "preferential option for the poor" and the importance of the church's commitment to social justice.

In El Salvador this preferential option became an integral part of the church's pastoral mission. Archbishop Oscar Romero criticized the government and oligarchy, claiming that it was not enough to undertake works of charity to alleviate the suffering of the poor; the church must work to transform the structures which create this suffering. The church continued to nurture the poor but in addition began to challenge the dominant society and to lend support to popular organizations committed to change. The church also helped form Christian unions. Political parties too responded to this atmosphere of hope, change and reform.

In 1980 five groups advocating an armed response to state terror formed the Farabundo Marti Liberation National Front (FMLN). Together with the Revolutionary Democratic Front (FDR), the FMLN made significant military and political gains in the early 1980s. The FMLN gained control over distinct parts of the countryside and spread its clandestine structure throughout the cities. The FMLN's progress alarmed the United States which then committed military materiel and advisors to the Salvadoran armed forces. In 1980 Archbishop Romero wrote to then-President Jimmy Carter asking for a cut-off of aid. Five weeks later Romero was dead—the victim of an assassin linked to the national guard.

During this time—the late 1970s and early 1980s—Roberto D'Aubuisson founded ARENA, the National Republican Alliance, an ultra-right political and paramilitary organization. D'Aubuisson and ARENA accept the division of Salvadoran society into the simple categories of producers and users. Law must favor the producers, D'Aubuisson has said, because they strengthen the "fatherland." ARENA is a nationalistic party and regards all "internationalists" (including church-workers) as enemies of El Salvador.

ARENA has characterized the church's preferential option for the poor as "communistic" and inimical to Salvadoran nationalism. This antagonism is rooted in ARENA's logic: capitalist producers are the foundation of Salvadoran society; any organization opposed to the forces of production is treasonous; the church's "option for the poor" favors non-producers over producers. The church is treasonous.

The late 1970s saw unleashed ARENA's "army of national salvation," the notorious death squads. The ten year reign of terror against the poor and their supporters had resulted in seventy-five thousand men, women and children killed—most by death squads with ties to the military, the oligarchy or ARENA.

The campaign against the rural population and the suppression of the popular organizations created massive unrest in El Salvador. Victims fled into San Salvador where they sought refuge in relocation communities or displaced-persons camps operated by the Catholic Church. There are three such relocation communities and one large refugee camp within the boundaries of Santa Lucia. Hence, the pastoral work at Santa Lucia can be understood as an act of rebellion against El Salvador's dehumanizing social system. The exact nature of this rebellion is evident in three activities of the pastoral team: the pastoral work with youth, the work with the refugee communities, and the work of the clinic and community health workers.

JUANITA MARTINEZ AND THE YOUTH OF SANTA LUCIA

Juanita oversees youth ministry at Santa Lucia. She views her responsibility as training young people for positions of leadership in the community. Some of the activities of the youth group are purely social: dances, outings and social gatherings of young men and women from other communities. But even these events challenge El

Salvador's status quo. The rules for Juanita's gatherings demand equal respect for women and men. Violence, including violent language and physical abuse, is not tolerated. The youth group often meets to pray and reflect on the causes of the violence which permeates their society and they confront one another to transform their lives and society to mitigate this violence.

In the course of these reflections the youth group at Santa Lucia has identified certain national values as sinful: individualism, *machismo*, conformity. They have likewise identified certain gospel values as necessary to humanize their national culture: solidarity, community, commitment. Language reflects reality and, particularly for the young, it helps shape that reality. Youth meetings in the parish at Santa Lucia have been condemned as "subversive." Juanita Martinez has been denounced as a guerrilla. Members of her youth group have been captured by the national guard, detained and tortured. But their work goes on.

This work includes organizing activities for the parish. The youth group provides dozens of teachers to the catechetical program in the parish. The youth are active in the liturgy, in parish gatherings and in work on behalf of the poor. One youth group initiative which began as an attempt to landscape the area around the church has developed into a very active ecology team. This group has secured permission to use a small plot of land to develop a nursery and a community garden of medicinal plants. They have learned that a commitment to the environment also demands a commitment to community. Their talk about a "collaborative" approach to the environment, "community" decision making for planting and harvesting, and *pastoral conjunto*, "working together," has garnered the ecology team and the youth group more suspicion in a society which considers collaboration, community and *conjunto* as sure signs of subversion.

Some members of the youth group are members of base communities. Some have a relationship with popular organizations. Some participate in protests and demonstrations against the government. But these activities are never organized by the parish or endorsed by Juanita Martinez. This is because she believes in the fundamental right of youth to make their own options in life without pressure from the church. This commitment to freedom, the cornerstone of the pastoral strategy at Santa Lucia, is reflected in Juanita's pastoral counseling. She refuses to accept the social servitude of the poor, much less bless it. She encourages young people to pursue vocations which are subtly denied them. She celebrates a young man's decision to be a farm-laborer—if that is in fact his decision—but she refuses to accept that he must be a laborer.

When young people ask Juanita, "But who am I?" she responds, "You are who you may become." Laborers may become doctors and even employers of other laborers. Juanita is not a socialist, nor a capitalist. But her encouragement of the young has gotten her into some difficult situations in the past. In El Salvador, when one advocates education and study among people whom the oligarchy intends to be laborers, one is advocating rebellion.

TOÑITA SANCHEZ AND ADMINISTERING FOR EMPOWERMENT

Sister Toñita Sanchez is the superior of the Passionist community at Santa Lucia. Toñita is responsible for coordinating all pastoral work in the parish and administering the aid the church gives to the refugee settlements in the parish. One of these is the San Miguel community. The members of this refugee community are all peasants who formerly lived in a dependent and dehumanizing relationship to a wealthy landowner. Their lives depended upon the landowner's support. He leased them their land. He hired them at harvest time. He decided, in consultation with the local commander of the national guard troops, who was and was not a "subversive." When the army invaded the rural provinces of Chalatenango, La Paz and San Vicente in the early 1980s, the people fled and sought the protection of the church in San Salvador. Some of these, like the people of San Miguel, settled on church-owned land north of the capital and slowly rebuilt their lives.

The problem is that under the system used to create these "relocation settlements," the church merely replaced the old landowners. It literally owns the land under these people's homes. Aid to the communities was channeled through the parish. Church patronage kept the people in a state of dependence, no less than their previous landowners had done.

Toñita Sanchez has recognized this pitfall. "Friendship and solidarity are more important than power," she says. Toñita has worked to bring power to the people of San Miguel and to reduce her own involvement in their decision-making processes. With her help the people of San Miguel have created a relationship with a small church group in the United States. Aid from this parish goes directly to the community of San Miguel and with it the people have formed a small credit union. Such a project is hardly revolutionary. But freeing the people of San Miguel from the twenty percent monthly usury of money-lenders has had a revolutionary impact on San Miguel's economy and the self-esteem of its people.

Toñita has also helped form a carpentry project for the young people of San Miguel. She reluctantly accepted a position on the board of directors for this carpentry shop, but agreed to do so only if her tasks were limited to training some of the young people from the carpentry shop to take her place. Toñita Sanchez believes that one's nature is to be discovered in the fullness of one's potential. Any system that prevents a man or a woman from achieving this potential, whether because of race (national socialism), historical necessity (communism), one's relationship to the forces of production (capitalism) or paternalism (such as we find in church-based charity), is dehumanizing and must be withstood.

ELIZABETH SANTIAGO AND THE HEALTH TEAM

El Salvador's violence is pervasive. One of its most notorious forms is rampant sickness and the repression by the government when people organize for better health. Community health workers like Elizabeth Santiago engage in an act of resistance when they get medicines and health care to communities victimized by El Salvador's economic system.

Elizabeth is from the San Miguel refugee community where Toñita Sanchez works. Elizabeth learned her health-care skills while living for three years as a refugee in the basement of the archdiocesan seminary in San Salvador. When the Passionist sisters in Santa Lucia learned of Elizabeth's skills they encouraged her to recruit and train others and to establish a clinic in the parish. This clinic receives help from the archdiocese in the form of medicines and occasional visits from a doctor. In 1989 it served 15,000 men, women and children, most from outside of the parish.

People start to line up outside of the clinic at 5 A.M. Consultations begin at 7 and continue until the last patient leaves, usually by 2 P.M. Elizabeth performs diagnosis and delivers babies. She does laboratory analysis of stool samples and is qualified for minor surgery. But in Elizabeth's own estimation, her most important work is health education and community organizing.

"We have to face reality," Elizabeth says. "Our health problems cannot be solved with medicines that we buy or are donated from outside the country. What will we tell our sick people when there are no more donations of medicines, 'Now you must die'? We have to teach people to prevent sickness so that, in finding cures, we do not increase their dependence."

Elizabeth has worked closely with Juanita Martinez on the medicinal plant garden started by the youth group. "Our forests and countryside were once rich in medicines," she says. "Why did we stop using these when medicinal drugs were introduced to El Salvador? It is because of an attitude on the part of us all that if a thing is made by North Americans, it must be better. It might be better for North Americans if we buy these medicines, but it is not necessarily better for us to use them."

Such talk has gotten Elizabeth into some trouble with the authorities. In her work in the rural villages north of the capital, she speaks clearly and forcibly about such issues as economic dependence and community action for better health. For a period in early 1990 she was followed by a detail of national guardsmen when she made her community visits. The national guard increased surveillance of the clinic where Elizabeth works and sent a captain to make inquiries about Elizabeth from her neighbors. Given the national guard's propensity for violence and the startling number of community health workers in El Salvador who have been killed in the past ten years, these intimidation tactics had their desired effect. For a time, Elizabeth stopped her community visits. She grew increasingly abrupt and aggressive with visitors to the clinic. She suspended the classes in preventative health.

"Then I saw what was happening to me," she said. "Juanita talked with me, as did some of my co-workers. I saw that I was doing to others what was being done to me. It was a difficult decision but I recommitted myself to the values that our work represents. I am afraid, but I refuse to give in to my fear and stop working. My fear has made me less patient and sometimes I become angry with people. But when I feel my anger rising, I remove myself from the clinic and I take some time to calm down. It is not a good thing to transfer the oppression I am feeling onto others."

When Juanita met with Elizabeth to ask her if she wanted to end her relationship with the clinic, Elizabeth thought and then replied, "No. The clinic is about life. It's better to resist—even to death." Her work continues, not in San Miguel but with a chain of city clinics started after the cease-fire was announced.

CONCLUSION

Juanita, Toñita and Elizabeth identify their pastoral style as "accompaniment." "The church refuses to accept the oppression of the poor," Juanita says. "And even though we have few resources to give to the poor, we can offer ourselves. And so we must be with the poor, in their communities and sharing their dangers with them."

In November 1989 the Salvadoran armed forces invaded Santa Lucia. The Passionist Sisters and their fellow workers remained in the parish. Through the witness of the pastoral team at Santa Lucia, the church in El Salvador has reclaimed its right to identify itself as a community of prophets.

Juanita, Toñita and Elizabeth did not take up arms in El Salvador's war. They chose rebellion over revolution. Each of these women is skeptical of the FMLN and mistrusts a revolutionary movement which not only uses force to oppose oppression, but has justified violence with reference to "El Salvador's historical project." Theirs is an act of rebellion that recognizes an individual's limits as well as the limits of history. The rebel tries to establish the limits of history and in so doing define values common to all.

The pastoral workers at Santa Lucia speak of the church and the gospel "incarnated" in history. To be incarnated in history means to share responsibility for human progress, as Christ did. In this worldview, "human rights" mean the right to achieve the fullness of one's potential within community. To be incarnated in history means saying "no" to whatever relegates human beings to prison. To the poor of this small parish, the church offers great liberating potential. It is rebellion.

TALKING ABOUT THE "STRUGGLE"
In a Rural Village of Chalatenango

Salvadorans talk about many things and in many ways. They share news. They gossip. They exchange greetings and inquire after each other's health. Women talk about the rising prices of basic foods: corn, beans, oil and vegetables. Men talk about work, or, more likely, the lack of work. Boys talk about girls; girls about boys. Old people talk about who is sick and who has died. Teachers talk about their low pay. Students talk about teachers. And for twelve years, everybody talked about the war.

The way El Salvador's poor classes talked about the war—the words and phrases they chose and the meanings they imparted to these words—reveals much about their understanding of this conflict: its aesthetics, the relationship between its principal actors and its ethics. The glossary of words presented in this essay were culled from an evening conversation in a rural village in Chalatenango, a northern province of El Salvador that borders Honduras. Chalatenango's population is comprised largely of peasants who farm the landholdings of absentee landlords. Chalatenango was subjected to numerous military invasions throughout the war. Survivors of massacres fled to refugee camps in Honduras where some remained for up to ten years. Their return to Chalatenango began in 1986 and was largely completed in 1990. The peasants who participated in the discussion which contributed to this essay remained in Chalatenango throughout the invasions. They lease small parcels of land for their own use and work on the large coffee plantations during the months of November and December. For the most part, during the war they supported the Salvadoran resistance, the FMLN.

The discussion took place while we were seated on stools around a small wooden table. The only light came from the fire in the hearth and a candle that flickered in a niche in the wall nearby. The stove was of traditional Salvadoran peasant design: an earthen-topped table rest-ing on four sturdy legs cut from a pita tree. The top had two circular enclosures for the fire. One was covered with an eighteen inch diameter clay plate for cooking tortillas. The other had a small grill, on top of which sat a clay pot bubbling with sweet, Salvadoran coffee.

The style of conversation was also typically Salvadoran. It took place in hushed whispers and was accompanied by numerous gestures representing forbidden words. A turn of three fingers on the right hand, pointing up, indicated the guerrillas of the FMLN. A clenched fist, moved back and forth in a boxing-type of motion, meant the guerrillas gave the military a beating. A quick motion of the right hand across the throat indicated the guerrillas took a beating.

There were four of us who participated in this conversation: Santiago Garcia, a former FMLN lieutenant; his son-in-law, Alfredo, a former fighter in Santiago's squad until he was captured and sent to the political prison at Mariona; Alfredo's wife, Juanita, a medic who served for five years with the FMLN in Chalatenango before the birth of her daughter, Rosa Lidia; and me. Others were present, but did not speak. Santiago's wife, Noemi, moved between the fire and the water tank where she was washing a load of clothes. She was the lookout. She kept her eye on the door and we all kept an eye on Noemi. When she reached for her ear (the sign that an informer or a person of unknown sympathies was passing by) we fell silent. When anyone entered the family's small compound, Noemi's youngest son, Saúl, gave them a more-than-cordial greeting so that those of us by the fire would know who had entered the outer patio. Even the small children playing in the patio were aware of the need for security. It was no coincidence that when Noemi tugged at her earlobe, these children's playful voices raised a few decibels, rendering our conversation inaudible.

The style of Salvadoran talking tends toward the paranoid. But the great care taken by Santiago Garcia's family is understandable. Two of Santiago's sons were killed in El Salvador's war; one was assassinated in front of his home. Juanita's first husband was killed in the army's invasion of San Vicente. Her husband was not a combatant, he was a teacher. That did not save him from horrible torture at the hands of the treasury police or from death by beheading. So this family's precautions were warranted.

How did supporters of the Salvadoran resistance talk about the war? First, they seldom used the expression "war." They referred to the armed resistance as the struggle. The struggle meant more than armed combat. It referred to the effort to live. When this effort involved a cooperative action on behalf of all the poor, organizing (for example to demand higher wages or better working conditions) or any challenge to the status quo, it often brought the peasants and laborers into conflict with the wealthy, the military and government.

The purpose of struggle is normally to achieve victory. It is important to note that the poor seldom referred to a military triumph of the FMLN as a "victory." This word has a more powerful, eschatological sense of final victory. One still hears the phrase "the final victory of justice and peace," for example. The designation "victory" implies that there can be no peace in El Salvador until the underlying conditions that caused the war are changed.

The FMLN (Farabundo Marti National Liberation Front) was the organization of armed resistance in El Salvador. Sometimes referred to simply as "the Front," it is a union of five groups that fought to overthrow El Salvador's oligarchical-military government. In common parlance, the guerrillas of the FMLN were referred to as *los muchachos*, literally, "the boys." This designation was only used by persons sympathetic to the FMLN. A neutral designation would have been be "guerrillas" or "rebels"; a more pejorative reference—"terrorist."

Supporters of the Salvadoran resistance generally referred to the non-combatant population under the protection of the FMLN as the masses. In some instances "the masses" had a more limited reference—the non-combatant supporters of the FMLN. Arguably a Marxist category, it frequently raised the suspicions of North Americans whose own speech is highly influenced by a media which employs such expressions as "Marxist-Leninist guerrillas" and "left-wing political parties with ties to the Soviet Union and Cuba" in the most ominous and disparaging fashion.

These concerns are dispelled when one observes two facets of Salvadoran life. First, the designation "masses" fits the Salvadoran peasants' experience. They are not treated as individuals but as a mass. Peasants who venture to risk bringing a complaint before local civic authorities are often rebuked with an opening salvo of "You people," as if a horde had descended to make some extraordinary demand. Treated this way, the peasant uses the designation "masses" with ease.

Some of the "masses" incorporated into the struggle. This signifies a status of commitment to the FMLN or to a popular organization sympathetic to the FMLN. One incorporated for a wide variety of reasons and in a number of ways. Many of the poor and middle class were frustrated in their efforts to participate in El Salvador's political life (one in which centrist and progressive politicians are routinely assassinated). Some became incorporated after their families were massacred or their villages bombed and their only recourse was to join the FMLN. The process of incorporation depended on circumstances. In some parts of the country, clandestine classes were held with assigned political reading. In other places, one "learned" the vocabulary of incorporation over time and by participating in the work of the organization. Incorporation usually indicated a person had shown the willingness to take risks on behalf of the struggle. Such risk-taking merited the confidence of others incorporated into the struggle.

Not all those incorporated into the FMLN were armed guerrillas. Compas is an abbreviation for "companeros" or companions. The compas included men, women and children who worked in some capacity to support the FMLN. They may have carried supplies—medicines, food, clothing, boots—from government-controlled territory into guerrilla-controlled territory, or arms and ammunition from guerrilla territory into zones where the FMLN was planning an offensive. Some compas worked in field hospitals. Some were involved in political work, literacy campaigns, public health or pastoral work. Most worked in areas under FMLN control, although some participated in the struggle in territory controlled by the Salvadoran armed forces.

Territory under FMLN control was referred to as liberated territory or sometimes as the "zones." Technically speaking, the FMLN will retain control over these areas as a result of the peace accord. At times the zones have included large tracts of Chalatenango province in the north, parts of Cabanas, Cuscatlan and Usulatan, the volcanoes of San Vicente and Guazapa and the northern parts of Morazan province in the east. The question that many asked during the war was: "How liberated is society in the zone?" The FMLN was not immune from compromising its expressed values, usually under the rubric of wartime contingency. The FMLN was severely criticized by "America's Watch" for lack of due process in its courts. FMLN political authorities in Morazan were criticized by the pastoral team for exiling store owners who failed to comply with the prohibition against selling alcohol.

Despite these problems, there were significant, observable differences between life in the liberated zone and life in the rest of the country. The peasants had the right to organize and demand their rights. They did so and were paid more for their coffee-picking labor than those in non-liberated areas. Second, even though these areas were constantly subjected to attack from the air, there was considerably less danger from death squads, random arrest and imprisonment—all common occurrences in those parts of the country controlled by the Salvadoran armed forces.

Many Salvadorans are committed to effecting social change in their country through the popular organizations. A popular organization is a non-government controlled organization, normally created to give otherwise disenfranchised people a public voice and an opportunity to express their demands in solidarity with others. Some of the most significant popular organizations are: UNTS, a coalition of popular organizations that includes CRIPDES (an association of displaced people) and Co-Madres (the Committee of the Mothers of Disappeared, Assassinated and Tortured Political Prisoners); FENAS-TRAS, an organization of trade unions; SICAFE and INCAFE, coffee unions; and FEDECOOPADES, an association of cooperatives.

Cooperativists, union leaders and organizers for the popular organizations are among El Salvador's "valiant ones." When Santiago and his family spoke of these organizations and their members, their hushed voices communicated awe and respect. These are the men and women who have taken the "struggle" into the streets, yet without the benefit of arms or shield. It is to protect these "valiant ones" and to "open up space" for the democratic process that Santiago, his wife, sons, daughters and their husbands incorporated into the FMLN.

CONCLUSION

A people's speech provides insights into how they view the world, how they organize its constituent parts and what values they profess. The speech of Salvadoran peasants "incorporated" in some fashion into the FMLN displays some important characteristics. When talking about their dreams and aspirations—their vision of a society of justice and peace—they demonstrate flexibility, adaptability and openness to the opinions of others. Their metaphors are just as likely drawn from religious sources as from Marxist texts. Neither categories are regarded as dogmatic or pre-ordained in the "historical" order of things. These same peasants exhibit considerably less flexibility in their language and thinking about the oligarchy and military. Here, Marxist concepts of oppression, class war, domination and imperialism more perfectly match their experience. The ignoble irony is that peasants who have clamored for greater opportunities for private ownership of land, the freedom to compete economically and the right to address structural problems in their society through democratic means have found meaning in Marxist categories. The irony lies in the fact that these categories have been made credible by an oligarchy and military which is, in effect, a textbook case of the kind of feudal economy criticized by Marx.

Part Three:
KAIROS EL SALVADOR

> Central America has become a *kairos* of unforeseeable conse-
> quences: either we close the door on the possibility of hope for
> the poor for many years, or as prophets we open up a new day for
> humanity and thus the Church.
>
> *Kairos* Document (Central America)

Salvadoran people express their faith in traditional ways, such as praying the rosary and singing devotional songs to Mary. Faith is also
expressed in new forms of worship, prayer and witness. In both cases
we have much to learn from the people of El Salvador—how they have
breathed new life into old traditions and created new expressions of
faith. Instances of both forms of renewal are described in "Part Three:
Kairos El Salvador."

During his brief tenure as archbishop of San Salvador Oscar
Romero was ever-present to his people and a source of strength in
their struggle for peace with justice. Although killed by an assassin's
bullet in 1980, Romero still lives through the church of San Salvador.
Efforts to celebrate the memory of Archbishop Romero similarly fall
into one of the two paradigms described above: through traditional
means—such as the elevation of his cause for beatification—and in
new, creative impulses from the Christian base communities.

The style in which Salvadorans express their faith does not trans-
late well into English. The songs they sing often seem peculiar when
sung in middle-income parishes in the United States. Those who have
visited El Salvador have learned this. Their experience in El Salvador
may have been powerful, challenging and inspiring. But it is difficult
to communicate this experience to the members of their communities
in the United States. This problem is one of the many faced by mis-

sionaries in the context of the new evangelization: how to share the faith experience of another culture with their own.

While acknowledging these difficulties, those of us who have visited or worked in El Salvador feel compelled to give witness to the *Kairos* of the Salvadoran people. Such witness is not an option. It is demanded by the gospel. What is this witness? To announce the good news of salvation and to denounce evil. Such witness contributes to the salvation of the North American church, which in the past and in certain circles often has been silent in the face of injustice. It also contributes to the peace in Central America, for, as many believe, the only thing that prevents the military and oligarchy from unleashing another great killing on the poor is the recently generated vigilance of the North American church for Central America and the possible economic boycott that such a massacre could evoke.

THE ROMERO MIRACLE

In the Catholic tradition the process of canonization involves a lengthy investigation, including the submission of evidence of some miraculous event—usually a cure from an incurable illness, restoration of sight or hearing—attributed to the intercession of the candidate. After one approved miracle (fully scrutinized by theologians, psychologists, scientists and doctors) the candidate may be elevated to the status of beatified. After two additional proven miracles, the candidate may be approved for canonization by the pope. In the case of a martyr, only two miracles are required.

Miracles are instances of change beyond a culture's understanding of how change naturally occurs. The Catholic magisterium regards miracles as a divine pedagogy. Through miracles God demonstrates mastery, not necessarily over nature, but over science. Miracles challenge human efforts to categorize and explain. They thus have an ironic quality. They express as much doubt as faith: doubt in the security of human paradigms, faith in a divine wisdom greater than these paradigms' ability to explain.

Normally miracles are instances of extraordinary change in the natural world. But why not social miracles—changes in the social world in a way that defies known paradigms of human behavior? Evidence of such miraculous intervention of God in history is evident in El Salvador. One may cite many examples. Most distinctive of all is God's vindication of Oscar Arnulfo Romero, worked through the great sign of El Salvador's Christian base communities.

"*Como Monseñor*" is an expression frequently heard in the poor communities of El Salvador. It means "like Monsignor," a reference to slain Archbishop Oscar Romero. This expression is commonly used in situations which defy common sense and "laws" of human behavior. Frequently heard in meetings of Christian base communities, "*como Monseñor*" expresses the miraculous (contrary to the laws of social behavior and common sense) intervention of Oscar Romero in the lives of the poor.

A "Christian base community" is a social type as well as a pedagogy. Christian base communities were formed in El Salvador twenty years ago as a response to the Second Vatican Council's call for the church to become more open to the world. In the intervening twenty years, this model has also been adopted by the Lutheran and Episcopalian churches in El Salvador, and by some Baptist churches there as well. Base communities are small. Their leaders are ordinarily lay persons, although their meetings frequently involve the participation of a priest, pastor or religious woman. They are intentional communities and commonly meet once a week in the home of one of the members.

"Base community" also refers to pedagogical process. Their focus of study is generally the Bible. Members alternate the leadership of their meetings. Leaders are responsible for studying the text to be discussed in the weekly meeting. The leader is also responsible for preparing questions for discussion, for motivating all the members to participate in the discussion of the text and for synthesizing that discussion.

Most of the participants are peasants, many of whom are illiterate or barely literate. How then do they prepare for meetings of the base communities? They may visit a priest, pastor or nun and ask for assistance. The Latin American Bible contains excellent scholarly references and commentary. The archdiocese of San Salvador has also prepared sophisticated study guides in simple language with lessons illustrated in cartoon characters. These kinds of material are considered "subversive" by many in the military and oligarchy. Materials of this sort were submitted by Senator Denton of Alabama to the Select Subcommittee on Terrorism during its investigation of liberation theology as proof of the church's subversion of democracy.

Members of the base communities are expected to contribute to the discussion of the text. They do this by amplifying its meaning by comparing it to their own experiences of life. In this the Catholic and progressive Protestant churches differ from the evangelical churches and Jehovah Witnesses in their approach to the Bible.

The evangelical churches and Witnesses use scripture in a conscious effort to promote a conservative ideology. When they enter into a community to speak, they are less likely to testify to their own faith than to use scriptural passages to criticize Catholicism or to make an argument against the FMLN, the unions or popular organizations.

The "progressive" churches' reading is likewise influenced by their unique perspective. That ideology is: salvation takes place in history, hence faith cannot remain separate from social commitment and action. Saying that faith demands a commitment to justice, particularly in a society like El Salvador's, also suggests that faith demands change. For this reason, the "progressive" churches have suffered at the hands of the military and oligarchical establishment in El Salvador. The military regards anything critical of the status quo as subversion.

The church itself is careful to distinguish political activity from evangelization. For this reason, and in order to safeguard their relationship to the church, El Salvador's Catholic base communities separate their liturgical and pedagogical activities from social action. While such separation satisfies the bishop, the military and oligarchy remain cognizant of what underlies much of the social unrest in El Salvador: the scriptures studied and read from the ideological perspective that faith demands action.

IN THE UPPER ROOM WITH THE
SAN JOSÉ CHRISTIAN BASE COMMUNITY

The San José Christian base community was formed in 1987. Its first meeting included representatives from four poor households. Few of the participants had any experience in the peace movement, unions, or with human rights groups advocating social change. At the conclusion of its second year of meeting, the San José community had swelled to forty households. Many of its members had become active in marches sponsored by the Permanent Committee of the National Debate for Peace. Others had become active in organizations working for peace. At the beginning of its third year the San José community had grown so large that meetings had become difficult and dangerous. The community was in the process of discussing dividing into two groups when the Salvadoran resistance, the FMLN, launched its offensive across El Salvador.

In response to this offensive the ARENA government suspended article seven of the Salvadoran constitution. Gatherings of more than three persons were deemed illegal. While exceptions were allowed in practice for religious services, the military made it very clear it did not regard meetings of base communities as within the purview of religious observance. Religion is viewed by the military as concern for the afterlife, whereas politics concerns things of a social nature. According to this understanding, the base communities were political gatherings and hence could not meet. If discovered, those who met could be accused of "anti-government" activities. They could then be arrested and detained without trial. Although the government had turned back the FMLN by December 1, 1989, martial law was extended into January 1990, then February, then March, then April. When the San José community met in early March to discuss its future, its members were fully cognizant that their assembly was illegal and that if detected by one of the many military patrols passing through their area, they would be arrested or killed.

The nun who had worked with the San José community opened the meeting with an attempt to calm people's nerves. "This really isn't a meeting," she said. "We're just here for a short time to discuss if we should meet again. Martial law is still in effect," she added, "and..." The pause said more than words could express.

The community was quiet at first. Each member realized full well the consequences of the nun's unfinished sentence. Then Emilio, a fifty year old farmer, spoke up. Unlike most of those who attended this meeting, Emilio owns his land—about eight acres. This hardly makes Emilio wealthy, but his independence from the caprice of the large landowners places him in a distinct social class from those who must lease their land every year.

"We should meet," Emilio said. "As Monseñor said, Christ is found in community. If we don't meet how will we ever encounter Christ? How will we learn about one another? Before we formed our community, whenever I passed Doña Mercedes on the road, I wouldn't talk to her and she'd lower her eyes from me. Yet, two weeks ago, Mercedes was married in the church and I was invited into her home to celebrate with her and her family. If we had not met in our community, how would I have had the good fortune to meet Mercedes?"

Mercedes is a peasant who rents land from a wealthy landowner. Mercedes' home is near a hill that is frequently bombed by the Salvadoran air force. The landowner lives in Miami but collects rental monies from hundreds of peasants like Mercedes through agents in San Salvador.

"It is true what Emilio has said," Mercedes added. "We should meet. As Monseñor said, our strength lies in the church, in community." She then recounted some of her experiences of the community. Mercedes was followed by others who recalled how they had struggled in the community to overcome their lack of confidence. Many commented on the self-esteem they had gained simply as a result of being asked their opinion and having that opinion respected. Although the members of the San José community were recalling their good experiences together, this discussion felt much like a wake at which people recall the best qualities of the deceased, forgetting the bad.

This mournful reverie was abruptly interrupted by a young woman who had remained silent throughout the meeting. "I have to say that I am afraid." She held up an infant she was nursing and added, "If we encounter difficulties with the authorities, who will take care of my baby? Will I be able to take him into Ilopango (the women's political prison) with me?" Her words hung over the group. She continued, "Like Monseñor, I'm afraid. But that doesn't mean I want our community to cease. You all remember the homily Monseñor gave the week before he died. He was afraid. But he went on. I think we should meet, but I think we should plan how to meet and also deal with these dangers."

She then opened her Latin American Bible to the Acts of the Apostles and read from Chapter 1, verses 12-14:

> After that they returned to Jerusalem from the mount called Olivet near Jerusalem—a mere sabbath's journey away. Entering the city, they went to the upstairs room where they were staying.... Together they devoted themselves to constant prayer. There were some women in their company, and Mary the mother of Jesus, and his brothers.

"The upper room was a place of security for the early Christians," she said. "They were afraid, just as we are afraid. And they had reason to fear." She continued. "Look! In the few chapters that follow, Peter and John were arrested and Stephen was killed. We have their example to follow as well as that of Monseñor Romero. But we also know that, because our cause is just, we will triumph in the end. Our commitment must be strong, but it must also be made with complete awareness of the consequences. In this the church in El Salvador has the model, not only of Mary, the Mother of Jesus and the apostles, but of Monseñor Romero. We know that, like us, Monseñor was afraid of the military. He was afraid of being tortured. And just as I am afraid for my child, Monseñor feared for us. But Monseñor did not let his fear deter him from his path; likewise, our fear cannot stop us from accepting ours."

The twenty members of the community present at this meeting then took turns acknowledging their fears. As the meeting continued, the people planned how to re-establish contact with the members of their network and how and when to meet during the period of martial law.

CONCLUSION

During the brief meeting described above, members of the San José community made continual references to slain Archbishop Oscar Romero. Most frequently they used the expression, "*como Monseñor,*" "like Monsignor." They asked themselves difficult questions about what Romero would expect of them today. They challenged each other, "Why did Monseñor die, if we now lack the courage to act?" They encouraged one another with Romero's words. They drew from their memory of Romero and what they had been told about him to gather the strength and courage to continue their process of reflecting together.

The San José community has been meeting regularly since this meeting that "really was not a meeting." Three members of the San José community have helped launch a base community in a neighboring village, an effort that costs considerable time and involves great danger. From March 22-24 four members of the San José community participated in a *triduum* to commemorate the tenth anniversary of the death of Oscar Romero. At this *triduum* Mercedes testified to her belief that Oscar Romero is with God. "I have no doubts," she said. "And the proof is here in this assembly. Where else would we find the strength to carry on, if Monseñor were not aiding us from heaven? Yes, Monseñor is with God, and we are with Monseñor."

Fifty additional members of the San José community traveled to the capital on March 24, 1990 to demonstrate for peace and join Mercedes and the others in the tenth anniversary celebrations in the Metropolitan Cathedral. The path of the San José community promises to be difficult. Two of its members were arrested and detained by El Salvador's national police after returning home from the Romero celebrations. The fledgling community which they helped to form was held under observation by a known national guard informant, now allegedly working for the national police. But the Romero miracle has proven stronger than the intimidation of the *guardia* or the dread of arrest, torture or disappearance. The memory of Romero lives in the communities and continues to give strength to the church in its resolve to struggle for peace with justice in El Salvador.

THE VENERATION OF OSCAR ARNULFO ROMERO

On March 24, 1979, a red, four-door Volkswagen approached the Carmelite chapel at Divine Providence Hospital in San Salvador. The driver was Amado Garay, chauffeur to Captain Alvaro Saravia of the Salvadoran national guard, and associate of Roberto D'Aubuisson, head of the ARENA party. Earlier Saravia had ordered Garay to transport Hector Regalado to the hospital, wait for Regalado, and then to drive him back to the city. Garay feigned repairing the car while Regalado approached the front door of the chapel, took careful aim and shot Archbishop Oscar Arnulfo Romero in the throat. At the time, the archbishop was standing behind the altar preparing the gifts for the offertory. Romero fell "like the just ones" of the Old Testament, "between the temple building and the altar" (Mt 23:35). His blood spread across his violet vestments and spilled onto the marble floor of the sanctuary.

In El Salvador, remembering Romero is dangerous. This is because the values that Romero advocated—reconciliation, peace, social justice—have become permanently associated with his life. To recall this life is to recall these values. For this reason soldiers of the Salvadoran national guard frequently seized pictures of Romero and literature by or about him when they entered a community to search for "subversives." Despite this persecution and dangers, Romero's memory has become part of the popular religious consciousness of El Salvador. This is especially evident in pilgrimages to his tomb and in public processions held in his honor.

PILGRIMAGES TO ROMERO'S TOMB

Pilgrimage is a form of remembrance which brings believers to the source and wellspring of their faith. Often the social experience of

100

a pilgrimage is regarded as disruptive to the status quo. This was true of first century Christians, and of the poor who comprised the pilgrim bands to Canterbury, and it is true of pilgrims to Romero's tomb today. Romero's body lies in the Metropolitan Cathedral in the heart of San Salvador. Before Archbishop Rivera Damas recommenced construction of the cathedral, Romero's tomb was in a nave to the right of the sanctuary. The coffin was entombed in a concrete sarcophagus covered with simple messages of thanks from the poor. On the wall overlooking the tomb was a large painting of the archbishop. This portrait shows all of the worry and concern that typified Romero's episcopacy. The nave was bare except for a few wood benches. People trickled into this nave throughout the day. They knelt to say a prayer and sit in silence under the looming visage of Monseñor Romero, saint of the Americas.

The cathedral lacked any worldly or aesthetic charm. Throughout the war it was of unfinished concrete. Steel reinforcing rods stuck out from the walls at odd angles. The windows were covered with corrugated plastic. Flickering fluorescent lights hung askew. The sanctuary itself was bounded by a huge wall of discolored plywood. Yet there was no mistaking the aura that permeated the cathedral and the tomb. It was a font of renewal, a holy place.

The holiness of Romero's tomb and the Metropolitan Cathedral must be understood in specifically Catholic terms. Catholic thought links salvation to the communion of saints in a reciprocal cycle of blessing. This notion opposes the Protestant, individualistic view of justification through faith alone. As Victor and Edith Turner argued in their masterful study of Christian pilgrimage, *Image and Pilgrimage in Christian Culture*, if one does not believe in the doctrine of the communion of saints, pilgrimage and associated rituals make no sense and decline in popularity.

Pilgrimage is a journey that culminates in an encounter with the holy. Rudolph Otto characterized the "holy" as *mysterium, tremendum et fascinans,* a mystery awe-inspiring and attractive. Pilgrimage to Romero's tomb in San Salvador's Metropolitan Cathedral is such a journey. When Salvadorans speak of "rights" they do so with the kind of reverence that most societies reserve for the holy. In El Salvador, justice and basic human rights lie outside the experience of the people (*tremendum*); yet they are part of people's longing (*fascinans*). Romero continues to symbolize this mystery and fascination for Salvadorans.

In a country where opposition newspapers are often closed, politicians assassinated and radio stations bombed, the Metropolitan

Cathedral became a place where the poor could hear the truth. Romero's homilies will never be esteemed for their literary merits but they were beacons of light and hope which emanated from the cathedral every week. Even today, it is principally from the church that the poor of El Salvador can expect justice; it is through the church that they can have their voices heard; it is in the cathedral that they can publicly gather with impunity. For this reason, the cathedral is a sacred place to believers and non-believers alike. The church objects when it is used by the left. For example, during the months of September and October 1989, a group of wounded combatants of the Salvadoran resistance took refuge in the cathedral and denied access to others. The Committee of the Mothers of the Disappeared, Assassinated and Tortured (Co-Madres) has done the same. Students have taken possession of the cathedral as have unions, associations of disenfranchised people, peasants and human rights groups. These seizures sometimes meet with threats by the archbishop to excommunicate the participants. His anger is justified. After all, what does it mean for a group to "seize" a sanctuary but to deny that sanctuary to others? But like the popular organizations, Rivera Damas has adapted to changing circumstances. He has not excommunicated these unlikely pilgrims and has advocated their rights, even when they occupy "his" cathedral.

PROCESSIONS IN ROMERO'S HONOR

In the middle ages the laity developed the religious procession to a high art form. Processions also made political statements. As in medieval Europe, so in El Salvador processions are sometimes indistinguishable from political marches. This may be why, ordinarily, the archdiocese does not officially participate in these and why it has done little to promote processions in honor of Romero.

But here again it is precisely because of the terrible conditions in El Salvador and the respect of the poor for the church that this ambiguity exists. Religious gatherings become forums for expressing faith in a saving God of history. Political manifestations and marches become opportunities to express their faith that these rights are ordained by God and safeguarded by the church. And in these religious processions and demonstrations the tired and uncertain visage of Oscar Romero figures prominently.

Demonstrations in San Salvador follow a specific route. They proceed down Roosevelt Avenue past Cuscatlan Park and the downtown market, ending in front of the cathedral. Marches are typically composed of between twenty and forty thousand people, chanting slogans, carrying placards and calling for an end to repression. During these marches, while the people control the streets, individuals will paint popular demands and aspirations on the walls along the route of the march—including the walls of government buildings. There were many such marches in the weeks before the 1989 elections. Not surprisingly, Romero's words often figured prominently among the slogans. The most common sayings were taken from the homily in which Romero said, "If they kill me, I will be resurrected in the Salvadoran people." Many variations of this promise also appeared, including: "Monseñor Romero lives in the struggle of the Salvadoran people," "Monseñor Romero lives in the memory of the Salvadoran people," and others.

Another favorite—and dangerous—place to write such sentiments is on the wall surrounding the American embassy. It is hard to imagine how people manage this. One is told: "It is done very quickly." Most of these writings were of a more specific nature, demanding the release of a particular labor leader, justice for the murder or disappearance of a teacher, an end to military aid and oppression. During the Holy Week 1989 marches the people did manage to scribble two Romero-associated writings on the embassy wall, however. One simply said, "Here they planned the death of Monseñor." The other was a quote from one of Romero's homilies: "The Glory of God is the poor who live!"

Many Salvadoran demonstrations end at Romero's tomb. In a sense this is appropriate since Romero's own conversion came about as a result of his involvement with the popular organizations. Furthermore, it was Romero's advocacy of their cause that gave the struggle for justice such great impetus. Visits to Romero's tomb are seldom an official part of these demonstrations. Ordinarily each of the participating popular organizations takes a turn making a brief statement of solidarity at the rallies held outside the cathedral. During this time people slip away to visit Romero's tomb, say a prayer and thank Monseñor for his sacrifice.

OSCAR ROMERO'S CAUSE FOR BEATIFICATION

Romero's memory has inspired annual celebrations, marches for peace and religious processions. Most of these have been organized by popular organizations with little official participation by the archdiocese. In 1990, however, Archbishop Rivera Damas stunned the Salvadoran church by officially submitting Romero's cause to the Vatican, thereby inaugurating his process of canonization. The months before this announcement had been distinguished only by their inactivity. The popular organizations and small Christian communities which had traditionally been the source of marches, liturgies and other events commemorating Romero's death had been restricted by the imposition of martial law. Three weeks before the anniversary, Archbishop Rivera Damas announced over the Catholic radio station that he was submitting Romero's cause to Rome for canonization. Ordinarily, the Vatican expects bishops not to submit names for canonization within fifty years of the candidate's death. The church desires that the process be measured and tranquil. Archbishop Rivera Damas' action was a significant exception. It unleashed a wave of renewed hope for peace in El Salvador.

In the few intervening weeks between the archbishop's announcement and Romero's anniversary the "Oscar Romero Society," an ecumenical group promoting Romero's cause, released a booklet of prayers for the way of the cross incorporating excerpts from Romero's homilies and published writings with traditional prayers. The archdiocese published a novena. Plans developed across El Salvador for local celebrations and also for delegations from small communities to travel to San Salvador for the tenth anniversary mass in the cathedral.

The archdiocesan celebration was carefully planned. On March 22, the archbishop inaugurated a *triduum* with theological content, prayer and personal testimonies. The first two days of this *triduum* were held in the chapel where Romero was killed. The final day was held in the cathedral. The *triduum* was attended by representatives of every parish in the archdiocese. It was also broadcast over the Catholic radio station.

The master of ceremonies who introduced the speakers on the first day of the *triduum* took pains to point out that the *triduum* was a religious and not a political event. The two days of talks were devoted to Romero's role as bishop and martyr and to his commitment to the church of El Salvador. Despite the dense theological language that typified these talks, there was no escaping their central theme: Romero promoted human integrity; he insisted that faith be consistent with social commitment; he was martyred for this belief.

The commemorative mass was an instance of this belief in action. Many people (estimates range from 12,000 to 24,000) gathered in Cuscatlan Park to join the members of the "Permanent Committee of the National Debate for Peace" in its procession to the cathedral. The National Debate for Peace was originally convened by Archbishop Rivera Damas. It is a forum of every major university and student group, churches, unions, small business associations, popular organizations and human rights groups. Conspicuously absent from the Permanent Committee of the National Debate for Peace are the conservative evangelical churches, Jehovah Witnesses and "private" universities. These were invited but declined to participate in such a forum for peace. After the National Debate drafted its initial position papers, its members formed a "permanent committee," naming Baptist Pastor Edgar Palacios as president.

When the permanent committee announced in San Salvador's newspapers its plans to process to the cathedral, the conservative newspapers condemned the procession as a political march. A spokesman for the national police announced that the march was illegal and promised to stop it. The day before the planned march, the national police, treasury police and national guard were seen practicing riot-control formations in the plaza in front of the cathedral. Such dire warnings did not deter the permanent committee. The memory of Romero fortified their resolve.

The cathedral was filled to capacity an hour before the mass was scheduled to begin at ten o'clock. Ten o'clock came and went but the archbishop's procession had not entered the cathedral. The master of ceremonies led the people in singing. A helicopter was heard flying over the cathedral and the tension inside mounted. People remembered Romero's funeral when the armed forces opened fire on the assembled mourners.

Suddenly a commotion was heard at the side door. The master of ceremonies nodded to the music director and the cathedral burst into song and applause, to greet the members of the permanent committee of the National Debate for Peace. Archbishop Rivera Damas had waited for the march to enter the cathedral plaza before entering his cathedral. The entrance procession for the Roman Catholic mass inaugurating the canonization process of Oscar Arnulfo Romero was led by Lutheran Bishop Medardo Gomez and Baptist Pastor Edgar Palacios.

The members of the permanent committee entered the sanctuary and formed a crescent around the main altar. The applause was now mixed with sobbing. All were on their feet waving, crying and calling out the names of the members of the permanent committee whom they recognized: Bishop Gomez, Pastor Palacios, Ruben Zamora, Guillermo Ungo. These names evoke the spirit of Romero; the anniversary of his death was the occasion which brought these men and women back to their country after months of exile following the Salvadoran government's brutal attack against the churches, unions and political parties.

Immediately following the members of the permanent committee came an entourage of Catholic priests and bishops from around the world. (Notably missing were many of El Salvador's conservative hierarchy.) Finally, San Salvador's Auxiliary Bishop Gregorio Rosa Chavez and Archbishop Arturo Rivera Damas entered the cathedral to a renewed burst of applause and tears.

Archbishop Rivera Damas' composure was stoic. Throughout the liturgy, which was broadcast to the thousands who remained outside of the cathedral, the archbishop showed no visible expression of emotion. He sat stolidly as each of the visiting bishops offered messages of solidarity from their churches. He appeared unaffected by the cheering of his church or by the tears of the people. While the archbishop's face remained a mystery to all, there was no mistaking the meaning of his words. Romero was a martyr in the great tradition of Christian martyrs because he dared to speak the truth. He is a saint because the particular truth he spoke was the gospel.

The next day the members of the permanent committee of the National Debate for Peace traveled to the province of Morazan to join in the celebration of the returned refugees from Honduras. These refugees had returned from years of exile to found a new town named after slain Jesuit Segundo Montes. The archbishop appeared on many of the television stations in El Salvador to talk about the ceremony. When asked by a reporter what he thought of the revitalization of the popular organizations, Archbishop Rivera announced that such work was a continuation of that begun by Oscar Arnulfo Romero, martyr of the Americas.

CONCLUSION: THE MIRACLE OF HOPE

Hope allows individuals or a society to search deep for hidden strength when everything seems to be going against them. Christians elevate hope, along with faith and love, to the status of a prime virtue. Yet, every virtue has its shadow. Popular Christian piety has often confused resignation for hope. But hope is not resignation. It is a commitment to continue to struggle even when things seem to warrant surrender. When hope flares, it allows human beings to overcome monstrous difficulties. It allows people to defy common sense and confound strategists. Hope experienced in the extreme, like faith and love, is miraculous.

A society without hope is a society of slaves. Peasant children who do not dream of being doctors and teachers are condemned to servitude. This is not to denigrate the work of a peasant. But the work of a peasant, like that of a doctor or teacher, should be an option in life and not a pre-determined chore. El Salvador's rulers and masters of war realize this. The immense power of the terror brought against El Salvador's poor by the oligarchy, military and death squads should not be underestimated. It is terror wielded with a purpose—to destroy hope—and with a definite economic end in sight—the bondage of the peasant and laboring classes.

Oscar Arnulfo Romero was a beacon of hope for the poor of El Salvador. For this reason, he was assassinated. Yet in death Romero has proved more confounding to the military and oligarchy than in life. His power to encourage and his ability to energize and evangelize seem with each passing year to grow, not wane. The effort to keep the image of Romero alive and in front of the people—like a beacon of hope—has fallen on many shoulders. These include local communities, popular organizations, human rights groups and the magisterium of the Catholic Church. Though uncoordinated in their various efforts and often at odds over methods and goals, the base communities, the popular organizations and the church have validated Romero's prophecy. He lives in the Salvadoran people. Through the devotion of the people and the celebration of Romero's great sacrifice, this saint of the Americas has kept hope alive in a country where it makes no sense to hope. "Like Monseñor," the people say, drawing on their memories of Romero. And they go on hoping.

MARY, A MODEL FOR LIBERATION

Many North Americans share the impression that traditional, Central American piety, by its very nature, inculcates passivity in the face of oppression. To cite anthropologist Clifford Geertz in defense of this proposition, traditional piety is a model of the social world, elevating social oppression to the level of the holy. But Geertz notes that religion has an ironic quality: it is also a model for an alternative social world. It both blesses and criticizes social life at the same time.

The cult of Mary in El Salvador presents an excellent case for Geertz' thesis. Mary is cited as a passive model for women, but she is held up as a model for liberation by many in the popular organizations. Considering Mary's liberating role in El Salvador requires understanding a basic cultural component of Salvadoran society—the effects of militarization. Militarization does not refer simply to the presence of soldiers, but to the attempt to impose military values, organization and world-view onto all sectors of Salvadoran society. In El Salvador many important administrative posts are held by military men. Through its officers' corps and retired officers' organization, El Salvador's military has exerted considerable influence over the courts, the educational system, the delivery of services (water, roads, electricity, communications, etc.) and the economy. In El Salvador, liberation means demilitarization.

MACHISMO AND MILITARIZATION

The brutal effects of militarization on Salvadoran society have been evident for the past sixty years. Until the mid-1970s the national guard units operating in the provinces of La Paz and San Vicente routinely swept through rural villages and city barrios gathering the blind, lame and mentally handicapped. Such "invalids" were not rounded up to provide them with social services. They were summarily killed.

Conventional wisdom holds that the national guard commanders of La Paz and San Vicente were proud of the reputations their provinces enjoyed for "cleanliness" and "productivity." These periodic "cleansings" were deemed necessary by the national guard, especially when the provinces were to be visited by foreign diplomats, potential investors, the bishop of San Vicente or other important persons who, in the estimation of the military, might be offended by the sight of such "sub-normal" disabled persons. Such "cleansings" ended in the early 1980s when the ascent of the Salvadoran resistance, the FMLN, demanded the full attention of the security forces. However, according to *Tutela Legal*, the legal aid office of the archdiocese of San Salvador, military operations under the control of government troops in these provinces still result in an unusually high death toll of disabled and aged people.

This forced eugenics is consistent with the ideology of the Salvadoran armed forces, an ideology which stresses the right of the strong to dominate the weak. It is expressed in excessive violence during routine military operations and, throughout the past decade, in a high incidence of rape by security forces. Reports of rape have increased recently. These document a terrible variety of cruelties reported by the victims—women, boys and young men.

The ruling ARENA Party in El Salvador has extended this ideology of domination into an economic policy. ARENA politicians claim that one's worth is proportionately related to one's ability to contribute capital to the forces of production. A person with capital is worth more than one without. Men and women who contribute to the accumulation of profits are worth more than those who cannot so contribute. Those who cannot contribute to the economy in this way, and who at the same time fail to contribute labor, are without worth or right to life.

All of these tendencies are subsumed under the cultural category of "*machismo.*" *Machismo* is a cultural phenomenon whose implications are not adequately understood by North Americans. It is not the glorification of masculinity. It is the deification of brute strength and the celebration of violence expressed in a myriad of ways: homosexual and heterosexual rape, state terrorism, ritual, rhetoric, economics and politics.

While strands of *machismo* run throughout Salvadoran culture, Salvadoran men are not predisposed toward its extreme manifestations as are evident in the armed forces. This aberration of an aberration (military machismo) is forcibly inculcated in rituals of initiation throughout a recruit's training. They are too pervasive to be regarded as occasional deviations from the norm. Military deserters and former draftees, for example, have described rituals where their units were made to stand in a circle while their training sergeant slit the carteroid artery of a dog. As the heart continued to pump, the dog's blood was gathered in a pitcher and passed to the recruits to drink.

Young men who have been subjected to this ritual report that when this exercise induces vomiting, the offending party is forced to drink his own vomit mixed with blood. The worst disgrace in the whole event is to faint. Weak-hearted youth who faint are branded "women" or "fairies" until they can reclaim their "masculinity" through acts of *machismo*. Such acts are not only counter-cultural, they are anti-cultural. These rituals are often accompanied by drinking pure cane alcohol. They include eating raw or living flesh or simulating sex with an animal, sometimes a dog or pig, while one's comrades shout encouragement. These rituals erode the recruits' self esteem in addition to destroying their moral values. Rape, killing "communists" and massacring children is much easier after such psychological formation.

Salvadorans share our revulsion for such acts of depravity. But they do not express surprise when these events are reported by their sons. Indeed, all Salvadorans are witness to military brutality, albeit expressed in less dire ways. As the military extends its influence throughout Salvadoran society, *machista* attitudes are growing as well. The planning of the national economy shows little concern for the poor. The execution of public works favors the powerful. National programs favor the "private sector," a euphemism for the wealthy. In such a society, any recognition of the value of the weak, any affirmation of the virtues of the powerless, much less their rights, is considered subversive and revolutionary by the dominant powers.

REBELLION AGAINST *MACHISMO*

It is ironic that, confronted with this aberrant ideology, the FMLN and the Roman Catholic Church—traditionally unlikely partners—once again find themselves allies in advocating change. According to the FMLN, *machismo* is "counter-revolutionary," and not only a denigration of Salvadoran women, but offensive to the dignity of all men and women. Unlike many Latin American liberation movements, the FMLN regards the liberation of women as part of its political project. The consequences of this commitment are evident. Women have achieved political and military prominence in the FMLN zones of control in ways unknown in the rest of the country.

Rebellion against *machismo* is also evident in many "popular organizations" working for change in El Salvador outside the armed struggle. Some of these groups, for example the Committee of the Mothers of the Disappeared, Assassinated and Political Prisoners (Co-Madres), have had public disagreements with Archbishop Rivera Damas. Still, their members are drawn from communities nurtured by the Christian faith. Women in these groups continue to articulate their social goals with traditional religious symbols, including the Marian devotions so prevalent throughout Central America.

Co-Madres celebrates the Feast of Our Lady of Mount Carmel as a patronal feast. The gospel text the church uses for this feast day, July 16, is John 19:25-27: "Near the cross of Jesus there stood his mother, his mother's sister, Mary the wife of Clopas, and Mary Magdalene. Seeing his mother there with the disciple whom he loved, Jesus said to his mother, 'Woman, there is your son.' In turn he said to the disciple, 'There is your mother.' From that hour onward, the disciple took her into his home."

In their interpretation of this text, Co-Madres does not focus on Jesus' parting words to his mother, but rather on Mary's *praxis.* Mary accompanied her son throughout his life and suffering, even when his closest (male) followers deserted him. Like Mary, the Committee of Mothers accompany their children who are imprisoned, or have been tortured or killed. They accept the dangers of this ministry of accompaniment. Their headquarters has been largely destroyed twice and many have been captured and killed for their witness. For the women of Co-Madres, Mary symbolizes, not passivity, but resistance. "Read the gospel of Luke," a Co-Madres spokeswomen recently urged a delegation of visiting North American church leaders. "Mary understood the consequences of poverty. She embraced life. She made a commitment to the poor and she demanded justice. She was not a defenseless woman who cried out for protection. She was a woman demanding dignity and compassion."

The popular devotion to Our Lady of Mount Carmel has its origin and *praxis* quite apart from the Co-Madres' program. It is one of the most popular Marian cults in Central America. According to Carmelite tradition, Mary appeared to St. Simon Stock, a thirteenth century prior of the monastery at Aylesford, England, and pledged to rejuvenate the Carmelite Order through her scapular promise. This promise was affirmed and amplified by Pope John XX who allegedly had a vision of Mary in which she pledged: "If men and women will wear the brown scapular (a simple brown cloth apron) in my honor, on the first Saturday after their death I will deliver them from purgatory." The scapular promise helped save the Carmelite Order from extinction. The devotion to Our Lady of Mount Carmel and the use of her brown scapular spread throughout Christendom.

The scapular soon became regarded as a magical talisman to save one from fiery punishment. It also came to symbolize a passive acceptance of suffering and injustice, promising, as it did, eventual freedom and happiness in the life to come. Such an attitude is hardly consistent with the progressive consciousness of Co-Madres and the organized efforts of the Salvadoran poor to resist the militarization of their society.

But the meaning of a tradition is neither bound by the intentions of its founder, nor by the social forces that have maintained it. "Tradition lives by grace of interpretation," Paul Ricoeur has written, "and it is at that price that it continues." El Salvador's poor communities are in the process of reinterpreting the scapular as a symbol of justification for their struggle against militarization.

Consider, for example, the contemporary interpretation of the scapular promise offered by Rosa Lopez, a catechist who works in a parish north of the capital of San Salvador. "The scapular is not our ticket to heaven," Rosa said one day while leading a discussion on popular religiosity. "Rather, we know that our struggle to achieve basic human rights is a just one. We mothers know that what they do to our children is wrong. We know that when we denounce this evil, especially the evil of violence, we are in danger of being attacked and possibly killed. We wear the scapular of Our Lady of Mount Carmel as a public witness to the justice of our struggle. They can kill us, but we shall not die. We shall persevere and achieve the justice we deserve. We wear the scapular, not to show to Mary when we die, but to show to our oppressors, as we suffer and live."

Rosa knows suffering. She raised two sons in a one-room house made of bamboo and mud. In early 1987 one of these sons was captured by the national guard, tortured and imprisoned for a year. His crime: a personal dispute with a young man who had entered the national guard. Rosa accompanied her son throughout this difficult period by visiting him in prison. During this time she joined a base community and began the process of reassessing and integrating her life with her faith.

Some have questioned why such a reassessment is necessary. Why not join the struggle for justice without involving popular religious traditions, including the Marian cult? What such a critique fails to note is that "revolutionaries" like Rosa were, for the most part, raised in the church. Even while recognizing the danger of religious fatalism, many men and women who are committed to the revolutionary struggle harbor a faith often linked to memories of traditional religious practices. It is the need to integrate this faith, these memories and this religious culture with a contemporary outlook that has led to a reinterpretation of the Marian cult.

Some would claim that Rosa has been manipulated by the "left." As Salvadoran theologian Jon Sobrino has pointed out, "long before the church made an option for the poor, the poor made an option for the church." Rosa is not going to abandon her devotion to Our Lady of Mount Carmel because her son was captured, tortured and imprisoned for a year. But that experience has influenced her devotion to Carmel. This is consistent with basic, Catholic ecclesiology. According to *Lumen gentium*, the Latin American bishops' statements at Medellín and Puebla and numerous other magisterial teachings, the gospel is a seed planted in diverse soils. The church will grow and its traditions will change depending on the historical climate and cultural ethos of the people. El Salvador's culture is being poisoned by militarization. In this historical climate and cultural soil, Mary has emerged as a model of integrity. The Marian tradition challenges the Salvadoran military's image of the perfect man. It is not "the left" which has transformed Mary into a revolutionary model. She has emerged as such because of the brutal and dehumanizing effects of militarization on Salvadoran society.

The integration of religious nostalgia and present realities is evident in the songs people sing to Mary. One of the most popular is "The Maria of my Childhood." Its words recall the simpler days of childhood:

> When I was young, so very small,
> I remember kneeling next to my bed,
> Clasping my hands, and praying quickly,
> But I prayed as someone who loves.

> How quickly I prayed my "Hail Marys."
> And sometimes, when I was tired,
> I fell asleep while praying.
> But I slept as someone who loves.

"How I long for those days when I fell asleep, thinking of you," this song says. It continues: "I forgot about praying. I came home tired and irritable, and I forgot my former talks with you." "The Maria of My Childhood" testifies to the loss of faith and innocence. It also recognizes the greatness of Mary's love. "A mother never forgets her love—even for those who turn away from her," says the closing stanza:

> I still come home tired and irritable.
> But now I pray as I used to pray.
> I pray the same words as in my childhood.
> I sometimes forget,
> And sometimes I fall asleep
> But this doesn't matter
> Because my heart is with you.

This song is popular because it reflects the people's experience. It may even be classic in how it addresses the longing for the simpler days of childhood while recognizing the impossibility of returning there. "Maria of My Childhood" is often sung by children in the company of adults. Yet, while children and adults join in singing it, the adults appear the most affected.

When the poor look to their religious tradition for a model to help them survive the struggle of life, Mary stands out. She knew pregnancy outside of marriage. She knew flight from massacre. She knew oppression. She knew poverty. She too witnessed the torture and death of her son. The *kerygma* of El Salvador's Marian tradition expresses Salvadoran faith: faith in the face of hunger, exile, oppression and witnessing the martyrdom of one's children—all of which are common experiences for the poor of El Salvador but generally unknown to North Americans.

The longing for the simpler times is a perennial human aspiration. Songs like "The Maria of My Childhood" would find a receptive audience in North America. Many Salvadoran songs, however, while admired by North Americans, cannot be sung in English. It would sound terribly insincere and incongruous if middle-class North Americans were to sing out about their experience of hunger and exile and their commitment to the "struggle."

Another popular Marian hymn, "Mother of the Americas," hails Mary as "mother of the poor" and "mother of pilgrims." Latin America is a land "graced by her barefoot visits." The refrain of "Mother of the Americas" announces the dawn of a new day in Latin America:

America, awake! The light of a new day
Is dawning over your mountaintops.
The day of salvation is upon us.
The light of a new day is piercing
The darkness of nations.

Traditionally Latin American hymns tended to focus on the miraculous power of Mary to intervene in history and less on her role as an historical person. The new, popular ballads recognize Mary's mediatory role, but more often praise Mary for her role in history. These hymns are Christological. The second verse of "Mother of the Americas," for example, identifies Jesus' birth as that "light of the new day dawning over the mountains" of the Americas. Because of this birth, the weak have been given strength, the poor given riches, and slaves given their freedom.

Because Mary was a "mother who lived in poverty" she understands suffering. She understands hunger. She understands the longing for a world characterized by truth and love.

You who know this poverty, free us.
Free those who suffer the most.
Free us from the selfishness that impoverishes us.
Free us to share and so grow closer to our Father.

In her role as a model of liberation Mary challenges the model of feminine passivity which the Catholic Church has traditionally held up for women. Many popular hymns announce Mary as "liberator" and "prophet." One hymn simply lays claim to Mary as a "woman of the people." This hymn praises Mary for leading the people in "the struggle." Through her, God works miracles, the greatest of which is the empowerment of the poor.

Maria, humble peasant woman.
A woman of faith and commitment, Maria.
Maria. Your "yes" rings of love and sacrifice.
You give us life, Maria.

The traditional context in which these songs are sung merits consideration. In the month of May, for example, Salvadoran communities honor Mary with "The Flowers of May." Families hold prayer sessions in their homes in which scripture is read and discussions are held around themes relative to the life of Mary. The Flowers of May devotion includes elements such as collecting money to support the church, singing Marian hymns and reciting the rosary. After the rosary, coffee and cookies are served. Throughout, the people continue to sing popular Marian hymns and ballads.

The Flowers of May devotion builds community. It allows people to share not only their ideas and prayers, but their homes. The event creates the opportunity for neighbors who may have had a falling out to become reconciled. It is a lay devotion which provides men and women in the communities with the challenge of organization and leadership. Sometimes the practice brings men and women who have "fallen away" from their faith back into the church. Through its humanizing role within Salvadoran society, the practice of the Flowers of May presents an alternative model of social life to that set forth by the military.

CONCLUSION

The Salvadoran poor lack educational opportunities. What the state fails to provide by way of formal education is compensated through observation, discussion and analysis. The church has also contributed categories and metaphors to popular analysis. Here Mary has emerged, once again, in Central America as a model for human perfection. It is important to point out that in this Marian renewal, Mary is not seen as a model for motherhood, women or femininity in general. She has emerged as a model for men and women. She symbolizes commitment. In discussions in the base communities she has emerged as a model of balance between political activism and obedience to God's will. She is seen as a faithful witness and an active advocate of the poor. She represents the integration of faith and action, justice and prayer that the church holds up as its response to the dehumanization of El Salvador in the wake of the recent increase in militarization.

The Salvadoran Catholic Church is hardly revolutionary. But given the militarized context of Salvadoran society and its cultural consequences—*machismo*, institutionalized and legitimized violence, glorification of power and denigration of the powerless—Mary has emerged as a metaphor for liberating change. If this revitalization of the Marian tradition is successful it will contribute to stopping the spread of *machismo*. A culture which esteems Mary's compassion will not be inclined to legitimize violence and *machismo*. A culture which extols Mary as a model for liberation, a leader in the struggle and a woman of the people will hardly denigrate liberation, struggle and the people. Mary as *Theotokis,* Queen of Carmel, Lady of the Rosary, Mother of all Christians continues to live through the church. Now, added to her many other titles, is that of the Salvadoran peasant: *Maria, liberdadora,* Mary, Liberator.

LICE IN MY HAIR, LATE FOR DINNER, *DONDE VA?*
Religious Life in El Salvador

Religious life in North America has borrowed heavily from the language and values of therapy. Novices are challenged to "take care of their own needs," to "assume control over their lives" and not "to give power over themselves to others." The metaphors we live by reflect and form our values. And American religious values, like the metaphors of American life generally, draw heavily from capitalism and individualism. North American religious speak of relationships in terms of power and time as a commodity. "Time is money." "I can't waste any more time on this project." "I've spent more time on this than I can afford."

The effort to renew religious life, in many cases, involves an inherent conflict between one's religious tradition and the desire to be relevant. Going back to our sources often means recovering counter-cultural values that reject individualism and materialism. Yet, being relevant in North America means "buying into" these values—speaking about life as a supermarket and acting accordingly.

DONDE VA? WHERE ARE YOU GOING?

When religious men and women come into contact with the poor of El Salvador, changes occur at both the personal and the institutional level. I recall many occasions when a member of my religious community in New York was leaving the house and someone dared to inquire, "Where are you going?" The answer invariably quickly came back, "Out!" That is to say, "You don't need to ask and I don't need to tell you."

In El Salvador I occupied a house in a small community of displaced persons. The forty-five homes of Santa Marta are clustered around a common area used for meetings and prayer. The well is located on the edge of the village and serves as a font of water, gossip, news and opinion. The homes had been built in a two year, communal work-effort by the families that now occupied them. They are made of brick and are tin-roofed. Located on a former garbage dump, Santa Marta straddles a route that, during the war, was frequented by the armed forces of El Salvador and the FMLN. Our immediate neighbors were families of national guardsmen and a large hacienda that was guarded by army troops and a private security force of retired guardsmen.

To walk from my house to the village entrance required passing a dozen houses. Two days after settling into my new home I decided to take a bus trip into the city and look for a journalist friend. As I was leaving the village each of my neighbors called out, "*Donde va?*" "Where are you going?" I wanted to reply "Out." Instead I gave as an innocuous reply, "Downtown."

"And when will you return?" my neighbors asked.

"This afternoon," I replied.

"But at what hour," each persisted.

"At five o'clock," I said, annoyed now to have my "private space" intruded upon, my time and needs held up for public review.

I should note that I was feeling a strong need to get away for the day. My house, like all houses in Santa Marta, became very hot during the day. I had to leave my door open when I was home and that was interpreted by all the children as an invitation to visit. What the children wanted was to practice their few words of English on me. After two days of this—counting to ten and singing the alphabet song—I was ready for a break.

I took a bus into the capital, bought a *New York Times,* ate at Pizza Hut and visited my friend at his office. He invited me to dinner and we spent a pleasant hour after dinner exchanging news about friends and sharing impressions of El Salvador. At about seven-thirty I said goodbye to my friend and boarded a bus for home. I arrived home at nine in the evening.

It was raining when the bus driver announced the Santa Marta stop. From my seat in the back of the bus I could see that a crowd had gathered in the rain. Pitch torches hissed in the drizzle. Flashlights swept the faces of all the passengers disembarking at the bus stop. I was scared and debated leaving the bus. Then, one of the torch holders spotted me and called out my name. The whole crowd started to call out to me and I recognized my neighbors and friends from Santa Marta.

I stepped off the bus and asked what the commotion was all about. Ignoring my question, the president of Santa Marta's community council stepped forward and shined her flashlight in my face. Rosa Amelia, a very small woman, is a widow and mother of three. She is poor and makes her living as a tortilla-maker. While I never doubted the strength of her character, I had not come to regard her as particularly threatening, an impression I quickly revised.

"Where have you been?" she asked.

"Downtown," I replied. "I met a friend and we had dinner together."

"You said that you'd be back by five."

"Yes, I did. But I was distracted. I met a friend..."

"And who are we?" Rosa Amelia asked. "We're your community. We've been worried about you. We've been waiting here since six o'clock. It's dangerous here. The road to Santa Marta is dark. There are soldiers about. If you want to live here, you must learn to be responsible to the whole community."

With that, she turned around and led us up the hill into the village of Santa Marta.

"*Donde va?*" I ask now when somebody passes my house. They tell me and I remember. I answer when asked and it helps to know that people care enough to worry. The people of Santa Marta do not take vows of obedience to Rosa Amelia. However, they live accountable to the community or else they are asked to live elsewhere.

SOME THINGS YOU JUST CAN'T DO ALONE

When the rainy season ended I had another challenging experience in community life in Santa Marta. It was early December and we suffered an infestation of lice.

I had noticed mothers running their fingers through their children's heads, probing for the lice, catching them in their fingernails and crushing them. The older children performed this service for each other. Spouses did as well. Grandchildren helped grandparents. Living alone and fearing the need for such assistance, I bought the most expensive delousing shampoo I could find in a San Salvador pharmacy.

This shampoo came highly recommended and I was convinced I

would not catch lice. So, when my head started to itch, I assumed this was caused by dryness of scalp. When my probing fingers found hard, little balls in my hair I assumed they were grains of sand. When the grains of sand started to move in my fingers, I knew I had lice.

I visited a barber to have my hair cut short. The barber pointed out that I had lice. Embarrassed, I thanked him and bought some more shampoo. The lice returned. After an embarrassing incident at the archdiocesan chancery when, during an interview with the pastoral vicar, I found myself probing my scalp for lice, I decided to take an hour every morning delousing my head. Still to no avail.

In the second week of this affliction, I was walking past Rosa Amelia's house and she called me over to visit. "Would you like some coffee?" she asked.

"Thank you, yes," I responded and accepted a plastic mug with hot, sweet coffee.

We spoke about the anticipated Christmas mass and community party. We shared memories of Christmases past. We talked about the gifts we were going to share with the children, purchased from the sale of corn the previous August. As we spoke my fingers wandered through my scalp, on their search and destroy mission for lice. Rosa Amelia smiled at first, and then she laughed.

"Sit in front of me," she said, and I followed her instructions.

"I've been watching you for two weeks and wondering when you were going to learn that there are some things you just can't do alone, and one of these things is to delouse your head." She then started moving her fingers through my scalp, probing, digging and cleaning the lice and their larvae from my hair. Some children stopped to watch, but Rosa Amelia shooed them away. After an hour she stopped and said, "Wash your hair now and come back tomorrow. We should be able to get them all in a few days."

The problem of the village's infestation did not go away. Not only was this a task that could not be done alone, it required a structural response to the problem. The community council made the necessary and painful decision to use the money saved from the harvest— the funds designated for Christmas presents—to delouse each house. The problem then passed and we were free of these pests. The lesson stayed with me, though. "There are some things you just can't do by yourself." One of these is to delouse your hair, but as I was to learn over and over again in El Salvador, there are many other things as well.

INSERTION AMONG THE POOR AND RELIGIOUS RENEWAL

Borrowing a basic insight from social science: individuals are formed by societies, not the other way around. When religious congregations include insertion among the poor as a part of their religious formation, communities of the poor exert an influence on the character of the whole order. An essential component of religious renewal in El Salvador is the hermeneutic privilege of the poor. The hermeneutic privilege of the poor posits that scripture is the communication of God with the poor of history. The meaning of a religious text is not limited to the intentions of the author. The reader also contributes meaning to the text. Scripture scholars refer to these two perspectives as the world behind the text (that of the author) and the world in front of the text (that of the reader). The hermeneutic privilege of the poor acknowledges that because the word of God was offered to the poor of history, the poor today, because of their poverty, share a privileged understanding of that word in a way that critical-historical study cannot emulate.

The renewal of religious orders and congregations in El Salvador is taking place as religious insert themselves among the poor. Insertion includes sharing the dangers faced by poor communities, sharing lice in their hair, tossing sleeping mats down on earthen floors, drawing water from the same well and eating from the same common pot of beans and rice. Religious are learning how to be obedient and still maintain one's sense of dignity and adulthood. Theoretical discussions about the materially poor and the spiritually poor are seen as that—theory—when religious men and women insert themselves into the communities of the poor. A new meaning for chastity, one more concerned with love than modesty, is also learned when religious share humble houses with married men, women and their families.

Many of the practices of religious life are called into question when religious leave the "cloister" and become part of communities of the poor. Contemplation, for example, is an important religious practice that requires time, quiet and discipline. Contemplation requires a whole new methodology when one lives in a marginal community located on a train track. When religious men and women respond to the needs of the poor by living in their midst, they develop styles of prayer pertinent to these conditions. Not to do so is to exclude the poor from religious life.

Scripture sharing as a method of prayer and study must be modified when religious men and women live among the poor. How do we share the word of God in communities where many cannot read and the majority are functionally illiterate? I have participated in scripture sessions where it has taken the reader ten minutes to read a passage of ten verses. The poor are not lacking intelligence. But when articulating their ideas and feelings they often use non-verbal forms of expression. Some communities in El Salvador have developed the *socio-drama* as a form of analysis and presentation. Other communities use folk-artists to record ideas shared by members of a community in a scripture sharing session. Salvadorans often create poems and songs in these meetings. The lack of openness to this variety excludes the poor from religious life.

Worse, to insist that we have quiet space for contemplation and that members have the ability to read well prevents the poor from contributing their wisdom to religious communities. If the Salvadoran experience offers religious men and women a lesson, it is that renewal is an inevitable consequence of insertion and that insertion requires a disposition to change.

Some religious orders in El Salvador have embraced the theology of liberation as a theory without making these changes in lifestyle. In these cases the theology of liberation has become an ideology, an obfuscation of reality, and not a light shone on reality. Other religious in El Salvador, such as the Jesuits, have taken the liberation challenge seriously and have been transformed as a result and have transformed the world in which they live.

The Jesuits have done this without sacrificing their commitment to higher education. Jesuit seminarians study and at the same time are actively involved with communities of the poor. Two Jesuit seminarians, Raul Molina and Felipe Mendosa, worked for two years with a youth group in Santa Marta to build a carpentry shop. Learning to motivate and guide the young men and women who built this shop required Raul and Felipe to move into Santa Marta, to experience the pattern of life in the village, to understand how time was used in the community, and to learn about relationships among the youth and between the youth group and the adults in the community. They lugged rocks and bags of gravel up from the river to build the carpentry shop foundations. They carried cement blocks into the community and learned to mix mortar. When confronted with problems outside of their realm of knowledge, they consulted colleagues at the university studying engineering and architecture.

Shortly after the structure was completed, a squad of young

FMLN combatants passing through Santa Marta slept the night in the carpentry shop. It fell to the seminarians to seek out the FMLN leadership in the area and to secure their promise that no armed men and women would enter the shop. This required courage and commitment to the poor that could not be learned in a class at the university. Nor does such training come from the Jesuit novice master. It requires lived experience and insertion among the poor in body as well as in theory.

Raul Molina and Felipe Mendosa helped the young people of Santa Marta to dream. They carried block and rock. They defended the neutrality of the carpentry shop against the FMLN. And when things were just ready to swing into motion and the young people about to begin producing furniture, these two young men were transferred to Honduras. Santa Marta's carpenters are young people and not inclined to piety. But Santa Marta's carpentry shop bears the proud name of *Carpinteria Loyola* in homage to these Jesuit seminarians.

It is the early and radical insertion among the poor that has given the Society of Jesus its particular character in Central America. Raul and Felipe were not following a personal inclination through their work in Santa Marta. They were following their provincial formation process that makes such insertion mandatory. Some enter the Jesuit formation process and object to such strenuous measures. However, among Central American Jesuits, the commitment to social justice and struggle on behalf of the poor is not optional. It is an inherent part of Jesuit formation and gives the Jesuits in El Salvador a national role.

Or does it? A small carpentry shop is hardly an earth-shaking contribution to the Salvadoran national economy. But Raul and Felipe will continue their studies and may return to El Salvador to teach at the University of Central America. And when they do so, they will teach in a way that favors the poor.

The proof of the consequences to the Jesuits' preferential option for the poor is evidenced by the terrible killing that took place on November 16, 1989. The squadron of the Atlatacl battalion that murdered these Jesuits had no difficulty entering the campus of the University of Central America. Because of the campus' proximity to the headquarters of the Salvadoran high command, it fell within a special "security zone." The soldiers had to pass numerous academic and administrative buildings before they came to the Jesuit residence. Their mission was not to destroy or damage the university, only to change its character by killing the Jesuits who exercised such an influence over El Salvador. They entered the pastoral center, torched the library with a flamethrower and went directly to the dormitory to drag the priests out of their beds and execute them.

The crime has been described in other places. Journalists, human rights specialists and the Jesuits themselves have described the suspicious complicity of American involvement in the provisioning of the Atlatacl troops and in the cover-up that followed. We know of the lukewarm investigation and the claim by the Salvadoran court that higher authorities, not indicted, clearly had a role in the killing. The court has handed down its judgement and expectations are high that the president of El Salvador will grant a pardon to the guilty. These events express the lack of justice in El Salvador.

The Christian communities' and popular organizations' response to the Jesuits' killing tells the other side of the story—what happens when religious stop debating the "meaning" of poverty and opt to live among the poor. When religious make a preferential option for the poor, and include the poor as formators of the order, great changes take place.

The armed forces of El Salvador continued to bomb and shell the capital while the six priests were interred in the chapel at the University of Central America. This bombing did not prevent the poor from paying homage to the slain Jesuits for their sacrifice and commitment. The campus swelled with representatives from across El Salvador: men, women and children who crossed military lines of fire to pay their respects to Fathers Ellacuria, Martin-Barro, Montes, Moreno, Lopez and Lopez.

The homage of the poor continued. While the Salvadoran air force mounted its counter-offensive, thousands of Salvadoran refugees living in Honduras packed up their few belongings and, defying officials at the border, marched back into El Salvador. They named their new home after Father Segundo Montes. Months later, on February 11, 1990, the Salvadoran air force bombed the houses of refugees who had returned to Corral de Piedra in the province of Chalatenango. These returned refugees buried their dead, mostly children, and rededicated their town as *Communidad Ellacuria*. The refugees returning from Nicaragua to Jicaron in Aguilares named their community after Rutilio Grande, the first priest killed in the recent conflict, also a Jesuit. Other cooperatives, carpentry shops like that in Santa Marta, bakeries, agricultural coops and small communities have named themselves after the slain Jesuits. Like Romero, they continue to live through the faith of the Salvadoran people.

Talking about this faith in relation to the Jesuits is a lot like the discussion about the chicken and the egg: which came first? The Jesuits have never been accused of humility and I have never met one that denied his order's important contribution to the church of El Salvador. The Jesuits also know that what they have been able to give to the church, they first received from their insertion and commitment to the poor. Although great scholars are sometimes prone to the kind of hair-splitting that gives us the unflattering adjective "Jesuitical," they have interpreted the preferential option for the poor in absolutely clear categories. If I may summarize their logic, from my personal observations: The poor are all about us. They are those who die before their time. All that we do, we shall do for the benefit of the poor. We shall learn what benefits the poor from the poor themselves.

For many religious orders in El Salvador, "renewal" remains an abstraction. When these orders move from the preferential option for the poor to radical insertion among the poor, renewal takes place, with or without a program. And for communities committed to the gospel, renewal always leads to disruption of the social world, a disruption toward justice. This is why they kill Jesuits in El Salvador and why their names appear with such frequency across the Salvadoran landscape.

TALKING ABOUT "SALVATION"
At a Roman Catholic Mass

The church in Calle Real overlooks the Troncal Norte, the main high-way leading to the Hill of Guazapa and onto the Honduran border. Across the road from the church, on a small precipice, the Salvadoran national guard maintained an outpost throughout the war. In a country where the military has killed lay religious leaders, priests, nuns and even an archbishop, the placement of this national guard outpost had a special significance. Calle Real was a "conflictive zone." It was heavily patrolled by the national guard and "civilian defense force" and was strafed in November 1989 by the Salvadoran air force. Calle Real is also home to three relocation communities of displaced persons and is a center for church-based social services to a wide area north of San Salvador.

At the time of this writing, Calle Real had no resident priest. The parish was administered by a community of women religious and a dedicated team of lay people. Together they developed a social pastoral organization and an extensive catechetical program with outreach to many small rural communities.

Sunday mass at Calle Real was presided over by Monsignor Ricardo Urioste. Monsignor Urioste has been vicar of the archdiocese of San Salvador since the administration of Oscar Romero. He was one of Romero's closest confidants and was elected interim administrator by the archdiocesan synod after Romero's assassination. Urioste is a complex man. He has a progressive social outlook and tends to be conservative in his ecclesiology. Although outspoken in his criticism of the military, he always articulates his point of view within the parameters set by his archbishop. He exhibits a remarkable sensitivity and awareness toward the people of Calle Real, even though he was only able to be with them for a short time every Sunday. "Monsignor (Urioste) is like Monseñor (Romero)," the people in Calle Real claim

127

in what is perhaps the greatest compliment a Salvadoran peasant can pay a church leader.

Monsignor Urioste's homilies are well-prepared. He frequently calls on people in the congregation to comment on the scriptures. This is not token "dialogue." At times Urioste disagrees with people and invites them to defend their position. At other times he incorporates their insights into his homily.

The notes for this analysis were made in early March 1990 in the wake of the 1989 offensive and during the weeks preceding the tenth anniversary celebration of Oscar Romero's assassination. At this time, El Salvador was under martial law. The anticipated celebrations commemorating Romero's death and the announcement by Archbishop Rivera Damas that he was submitting Romero's cause to the Vatican for beatification influenced all the church, including Monsignor Urioste's homilies.

The word "prophet" figures prominently in Ricardo Urioste's homilies. His use is consistent with that in Hebrew scriptures. A prophet is not one who predicts the future. It is that man or woman who describes reality in a way that resonates with people's experience and who criticizes reality from the basis of a shared religious tradition. "The Salvadoran church is a church of prophets," Monsignor Urioste often reminds the people in Calle Real. "We all share in the responsibility to tell the truth as we see it, and to call each other to greater faith." The Roman Catholic archdiocese undertakes its "prophetic mission" in a number of important ways. Since the time of Romero, the archbishop's weekly homilies have included a section on the "national reality"—a commentary on the week's events. For many poor Salvadorans, the broadcast of this homily is the only formal source of information about national events. For this reason the archdiocesan radio station has been bombed three times. The archbishop also participates in a weekly press conference after the Sunday mass. In addition to the archdiocesan radio station, the archdiocese publishes *Orientacion,* a weekly newspaper. This prophetic tradition of relating the scriptures to social reality has become entrenched in many parishes, earning the Church the enmity of the military.

While Hebrew scriptures provide the Salvadoran church with its prophetic archetype, the life and episcopal ministry of slain Archbishop Oscar Romero is often cited by Monsignor Urioste as the prophetic paradigm. The expression "like Monseñor" exhorts the people of Calle Real to greater fidelity to the gospel. Romero was the voice of the voiceless. To be the voice of the voiceless is to speak the truth for the poor, whose voice is not heard by those who can bring about constructive change. Romero was considered the voice of the voiceless in El Salvador, but this responsibility is now assumed as co-equal with that of prophecy. To be the voice of the voiceless is therefore to be a prophet, "like Monseñor." In Urioste's March 1990 homilies he invited all the people of Calle Real to be the voice of the voiceless, to speak the truth for those who cannot be heard and to express their demands in the public forum. The fullest meaning of speech depends upon the relationship of the speaker to hearer and the relationship of both to the referent. Ten years after his death, Romero's relationship to the poor of El Salvador is as strong as it was during the archbishop's life. As mentioned above, the poor of Calle Real regard Monsignor Urioste as a faithful steward of the Romero legacy. Thus, when Urioste speaks of Monseñor Romero to the people of Calle Real, it is like old friends remembering. But more than nostalgia, Urioste invokes Romero's name to call the people of Calle Real to greater fidelity to the gospel, "like Monseñor." Urioste uses Romero's life and teachings to invite the community of Calle Real to examine their own, small culpability and responsibility for the violence and ruin permeating El Salvador.

Three words that often appear in Urioste's homilies are history, incarnation, and community. The Catholic faith is rooted in scripture but is historical as well. The church holds that its faith is part of history. The popular songs of the Salvadoran church proclaim, "History will not be silenced." While the God of Catholicism is a God of history—a God interested in the affairs of history—the church has not elevated history to the status of God. In this the church is significantly different from revolutionary Marxism which regards the revolution as an inevitable product of history. Rather, the church holds that men and women are part of history, are influenced by history, but have control over its course through the exercise of free will.

Incarnation expresses the central Catholic belief that God became human in the person of Jesus and "dwelt amongst us." The concept of incarnation is linked to that of history. Because God became human in the person of Jesus Christ, Catholic doctrine vitiates the dualism between matter and spirit. Teachers like Urioste stress the "integrity" of every human person. Holiness consists in the perfection of the total person. This certainly includes, but is not limited to, the spirit. Peace at heart is only possible when one also achieves peace in one's personal relations, peace in the family and peace in society.

Belief in the incarnation of God in history mandates that Christians work within history to create a more perfect social order. These two concepts—history and incarnation—place the Catholic Church in El Salvador at odds with the conservative oligarchy and military.

Community and community building are a central focus of the church's pastoral work. Sacraments are no longer given privately—for example, in the home or in the sacristy after mass. They are always celebrated within the community and include the whole community. Urioste constantly warns his congregation against the sin of "egoism." "What is egoism?" he asks. "It is the opposite of community." Egoism may be translated as selfishness, but it extends beyond personal behavior. "It is a structural condition that isolates people from one another, prohibits building community, and hinders the reign of God." The church's commitment to building community is exemplified by the social secretariat for the archdiocese of San Salvador. This office supervises the work of clinics, aid to refugees and displaced persons, work projects within the poor parishes of the archdiocese, and counseling and technical assistance to community groups.

The responsibility of building community based on Christian values is shared by the church.

Monsignor Urioste often uses natural and agricultural metaphors to talk about community building. The faith of the people is the fertile ground, he says. Faith is nourished by the rain of God's love. The seed that brings forth Christian community is the word of God.

In addition to the leadership of priests and nuns, the Salvadoran church relies heavily on the work of "delegates of the word" to plant the word of God. These are men and women from the community whose responsibility is sharing scripture with small groups in their communities and leading these people in discussion. The Catholic Church has been accused by some sectors of suppressing the study of the Bible. This criticism stems from the fact that the church jealously guards the teaching authority of the bishop (in collaboration with priests). The high educational requirements placed by the church on the laity who could preach the word are prohibitive and have made many Latin American churches dependent on mission support. But delegates of the word do not teach. They lead people in discussions of the scriptures and help these groups to apply scripture to their own reality. The goal, therefore, is not only to understand scripture better, but to better understand social life. In El Salvador such analysis is dangerous, and countless delegates of the word have been "disappeared" or been killed, often in the most horrible manner.

Perhaps the most misunderstood word in the church's lexicon is liberation. To fully understand it, one must examine the church's understanding of sin. Sin is anything which prohibits people from achieving the fullness of their human potential. The church recognizes personal sin as well as social sin. Poverty is a sin. Hunger is a sin. Conditions that lead to early death certainly limits one's human potential and so is a sin. Liberation is overcoming sin. Overcoming the social conditions that create poverty, hunger and early death is considered (with other acts) liberation. In the context of the oppressive social and economic reality of El Salvador, this vision has placed the church at loggerheads with the military establishment.

CONCLUSION

The key to understanding Monsignor Urioste's preaching is the word "salvation." In Catholic theology, the concept of salvation is used to signify the liberation from all conditions of bondage and need. This includes individual need as well as the needs of society. Monsignor Urioste is able to address the salvific needs of the people of Calle Real because his first principle of pastoral care is to listen. Indeed, he has listened to the poor of Calle Real, and the whole archdiocese, for a long time. When Monsignor Urioste talks about "salvation from the sin of greed" he addresses the greed to which all persons, rich and poor, are susceptible. When he preaches salvation from *machismo,* his images are drawn from the pornographic artwork that adorns buses. He has also attacked the more institutional form of *machismo* that permeates the military. When Monsignor Urioste preaches salvation from egoism, he speaks against the petty forms of selfishness as well as the structural prohibitions that militate against cooperation at the community level.

Monsignor Urioste's homilies on the miracle stories, his interpretation of the parables and his commentary on the Hebrew scriptures ring faintly traditional. He assures the people of Calle Real that God does intervene in history. He encourages people to pray for this intervention. He prays with them. And then he encourages them to work for their salvation with the same enthusiasm as when they prayed.

Monsignor Urioste is an advocate of change. The military—for obvious reasons—advocates the status quo. In this respect, the language of the church, when it is faithful to Catholic tradition, sometimes resembles that of FMLN supporters. The FMLN has called for the salvation of society, leading to a change in individuals. Church leaders like Monsignor Urioste have called for the salvation of individuals leading to change in society. Fundamentally, it is change itself that the military finds threatening and has labeled "communism."

The church has been criticized by the government for using the same language as the FMLN to address the structural problems in Salvadoran society. The FMLN has exploited this fact. In a January 1990 communiqué to the "bishops, priests, religious of the Catholic Church; bishops, ministers and pastors of the Lutheran, Baptist and Episcopal churches," the FMLN praised them: "Inspired by the gospel and following the example of Jesus, you have worked with and in the midst of our people, to advance the process of liberation and to construct now and later the reign of God." Citing scripture, this communiqué acknowledged Jesus' option for the poor. It acknowledged that the church's option for the poor has earned the wrath of the military. The FMLN did not try to gloss over its differences with the churches. "We respect these profound differences and acknowledge how important these are for a pluralist society." This communiqué ended with an acknowledgement that the followers of Jesus could not remain true to the gospel if they separated history from the gospels, and it commended the churches for their struggle to advance the freedom of the poor.

Part Four:
WANTING PEACE,
WORKING FOR JUSTICE

"If you want peace, work for justice."

Pope Paul VI

On September 15, 1991 the FMLN and the government of El Salvador issued a joint statement from United Nations headquarters in New York indicating that they were close to reaching consensus on key issues pertinent to a cease fire. On December 31, 1991 the date for the cease fire was announced–January 16, 1992. Shortly later, the details of the New York accords were announced in El Salvador.

The people of El Salvador have learned in the first difficult year since the signing of the peace accords that their struggle has not ended. It has simply changed playing fields. It has left the field of guns, bombs and land mines for that of organizing elections, cooperatives and the right to compete economically in world markets. The prophetic words of Pope Paul VI–"If you want peace, work for justice"–best describe the Salvadoran struggle. Paul VI's challenge is all the more important in post-war, pre-elections El Salvador. It has focused the church and energized the base communities. The peace accord did not create justice. It simply provides the possibility for Salvadorans to participate in the birthing of justice. The struggle ahead promises to be long and difficult.

What justice is sought in El Salvador? First, Salvadorans desire guarantees for basic human rights. This requires creating a civilian-controlled police force and a judicial system free of military control. Second, they want economic justice. This will invariably take the form of land reform, support for cooperativism and tax reform. Whatever it requires, Salvadorans must first institute a democratic process that guarantees the right of all to participate. And the United States must respect that process. Finally, Salvadorans want justice in the new world order. Like any developing nation, El Salvador must be given the support it needs to rebuild an economic infrastructure, free from international manipulation.

To achieve these goals, El Salvador requires the continued solidarity and accompaniment of all men and women committed to peace-building.

THE PEACE PROCESS IN EL SALVADOR
(A Hermeneutic of Suspicion)

On February 11, 1990 the Salvadoran air force bombed Corral de Piedra, a small community of returned refugees in the province of Chalatenango. The attack proceeded thus: At about 8:30 in the morning three Huey helicopters commenced strafing Corral de Piedra with machine-gun fire. They then let loose a barrage of rockets against the village and its environs. Later, two A-37 Dragonfly airplanes dropped eight bombs on Corral de Piedra. The attack lasted one hour.

Three houses received direct hits. The corrugated metal roofs and adobe walls offered minimal protection against flying shrapnel. Four children and one adult died immediately. Seventeen others required hospitalization for wounds sustained in the attack. The most horrible sight greeting the survivors was the lacerated and crushed body of two year old Blanca Guardado enveloped in the arms of her dead father, Jose.

The survivors who were ambulatory organized an evacuation of the wounded to the city of Chalatenango. During this evacuation the air force returned with two C-47 Dakotas and again strafed the village.

Corral de Piedra is not an extraordinary case. The list of massacres and attacks against defenseless civilians is a long one. Despite the fact that the government of El Salvador and the Salvadoran resistance, the FMLN, have negotiated this cease-fire, it is still important to recall the victims and the reason they died: Mogotes—31 killed; Guazapa—34 killed; Armenia—23 killed; Mozote—800 killed; San Antonio Abad—35 killed; San Jose Las Flores—57 killed; Sumpul River—600 killed; Los Cerros de San Pedro—300 killed.

The special, U.S.-trained Atlacatl battalion has its own list of massacres: Tenango and Guadalupe—150 killed; Tenancingo—50 killed; Copapayo—118 killed; Las Piletas, Gualsinga River—34 killed. At times the Atlacatl has joined forces with the Belloso battalion: San Carlos Lempa—25 killed; Los Llanitos—68 killed. The Atlacatl also participat-

135

ed in Operation Phoenix on Guazapa volcano where 245 civilians, mostly women and children, were killed. On November 16, 1989 soldiers of the Atlacatl battalion entered the Jesuit University of Central America and brutally killed six priests and two housekeepers.

Salvadorans long for assurances that these massacres will end. They know it is not enough to sign a document saying that "the Armed Forces and the FMLN will respect human rights." Such assurances have been offered in the past. Called, variously, "messages," "symbols," "indications" and "signs of peace," they have been ineffectual. Massacres are not the cause of El Salvador's problems; they are a consequence of larger injustices. The dialogue for peace must address the underlying causes of the conflict as well as their consequences.

INTERPRETING DEATH: SOME MODELS FROM EL SALVADOR

How can we understand such acts? Since 1932 the Salvadoran military and their wealthy patrons have justified warring on the poor as a defense against communism. It is true that the Salvadoran insurgency has included elements of the Salvadoran Communist Party and has received material assistance from Nicaragua, Cuba and the Soviet Union. But as El Salvador's president Alfredo Cristiani himself recently admitted, the causes of the war are inherent in El Salvador's economy and social structure. These conditions were exacerbated by the east-west conflict, not created by it. Ironically, the international symbol of communist hegemony, the Berlin wall, was torn down before our eyes on nightly television as the Atlacatl battalion was preparing to invade the UCA to kill the six Jesuits.

In some cases, like Corral de Piedra, the Salvadoran high command has accounted for massacres as accidents of war. And accidents do happen in war. But Corral de Piedra was no accident, nor was Mogotes, Guazapa, Armenia, Mozote, Las Flores, Los Cerros, the massacre at the UCA and all the rest. In El Salvador, massacre has become the norm for war-making. The pattern itself suggests a rationale, equating war with terrorism.

Some claim that the armed forces of El Salvador kill only for the pleasure of killing, because they are evil. This is an expression of the "Black Legend," the most ubiquitous interpretation for Latin American history heard in the United States. It goes like this: Killing is a Salvadoran cultural trait. Salvadorans are a naturally violent people.

They are hot-headed, hot-blooded and lacking any appreciation for democracy, human rights and peaceful mediation of differences.

Reference to the Black Legend belies the deeper rationale for making war on the poor. Military actions in El Salvador, like that at Corral de Piedra, were acts of terrorism. They were planned and executed in order to maintain the Salvadoran system of agricultural production by terrorizing the population and guaranteeing a ready and cheap supply of labor. The proof of this contention is, quite literally, evident across the Salvadoran landscape.

* * *

From early November until late January, in early mornings and late afternoons, Salvadoran highways are choked with lines of peasants—men, women and children—trekking to the plantations to pick coffee and cotton and to cut sugar cane.

Each coffee worker carries a basket and tumpline. These are not happy peasants, like the Juan Valdez of commercial fame. The children are malnourished and exhausted. The adults appear haggard. Coffee picking is tiresome work with little economic reward.

During these months, bales of cotton line the sides of the coastal highways. One can see lean-tos set among the cotton fields, temporary homes for the seasonal workers toiling under the sun.

Sugar cane is cut by hand. Sugar cane also cuts, lacerating the hands and arms of the men and women who wield machetes. Children haul the cane to waiting trucks. Exhausted after a few hours' work, they cannot pause to rest except at designated periods. The flow of profit cannot be disrupted.

The coastal highways are very dangerous during harvest time. Trucks brimming with sugar cane race from field to crusher and from crusher to refinery. Profit rules in El Salvador. There is no concern for the safety of the workers. These trucks are piled so high they often fall over, killing people on the road. All spew toxic fumes. This is harvest-time in El Salvador.

The three main export crops—cotton, sugar and coffee—must be harvested in November, December and January. All are labor intensive and require very little labor during the rest of the year. A lack of available labor during these months would mean losing the crop and thus El Salvador's second-largest source of foreign capital after the United States' contribution to the war effort. If the majority of people were gainfully employed in a stable economy, there would be no workers for the harvest. The Salvadoran export economy, therefore, depends as much on seasonal unemployment and underemployment (from February until October) as on available labor from November until January.

The wages from the harvest are low and are used to purchase clothing or shoes for the children and possibly a few Christmas presents. The peasants are paid piecemeal, and by the end of the harvest many workers spend more on the costs incurred to pick coffee than they earn. Why would they continue to work? For the coffee pickers, gleaning rights belong to those who stay for the whole harvest. Also, some plantations refuse to rehire peasants who work only during the more profitable early part of the season.

The export economy of El Salvador is weakened by competition from crops cultivated for local consumption. The staples of the Salvadoran diet are corn and beans. Corn is planted, usually on leased land, in early May. The corn ripens in August and some is harvested. The majority of the corn cobs, however, are snapped while on the stalk, allowed to dry in the field and picked throughout October and November. The bean crop is planted in September alongside the rows of corn. The beans are harvested in November and December. Thus, El Salvador's three main export crops—its source of foreign capital—and its two important domestic crops—the dietary staple of the poor—are all harvested in the same season. The corn and bean harvests are more important to the peasant than the coffee, cotton and sugar harvests. The motivation to pick coffee is undermined, not only by low wages, but by the relative lack of importance of the crop in the life of the poor.

Salvadoran peasants have long realized how easy it would be to demand higher wages if they were organized. If workers had the right to organize and to strike, the agricultural economy would favor workers over producers. Coffee beans, for example, ripen at different times throughout the harvest, and the export-quality beans must be picked before they fall to the ground. A two week strike would cost the landowners dearly. If there are no pickers, there is no harvest. If there is no harvest, there is no foreign exchange for the government and oligarchy.

Until El Salvador diversifies its economy and restructures the relationship of the workers to the landowners, allowing greater participation from all levels of society in decision-making, it will be torn by civil and class war.

* * *

How did El Salvador's economy develop in such a precarious fashion? Soon after the conquest, the central region of El Salvador was organized in colonial plantations that grew trade-crops of balsam, cacao and indigo. But partly as a consequence of El Salvador's isolation, large-scale development was delayed. The Spanish permitted the Indians to maintain much of their traditional system of communal lands. Nuclear families maintained gardens close to home for fresh fruits and vegetables. Large, extended families used fields for common grazing, cultivation of staples and some crops for sale. The extended families adapted a saint as protector and used the saint's feast day as an annual celebration and opportunity to review communal leadership. These communes, like contemporary Salvadoran agricultural cooperatives, were not principally organized for export production, but to grow crops for local consumption.

Central America became independent from Spain in 1821. A loose Central American Union floundered until 1839 at which time El Salvador and the other countries of Central America became independent from one another. During these years the landed oligarchy initiated efforts to dissolve the Indian communal lands. In 1833 this contributed to an uprising led by Anastasio Aquino. The landowners suppressed the uprising and advanced the program to dissolve communal lands.

During these years, the Salvadoran government secured most of its operating revenue from export taxes on indigo. In the 1850s the government became alarmed by the decline in demand for indigo. Wishing to diversify and expand its source of foreign capital, the oligarchal families again proposed privatizing the Indians' communal lands to increase export production. This "bourgeois revolution" culminated in the constitution of 1886. Communal lands were offered for sale. The only families who had the cash to purchase these lands were those who had written the constitution. As a result, large tracts of land that had been farmed for internal production were turned over to cash crops—indigo, cotton, sugar and coffee. The Indians were required to lease lands from the new landowners. The Indians' only source of cash was to work as seasonal laborers on the newly enlarged plantations. The privatization of lands was seen by the Salvadoran oligarchy as the only way to bring El Salvador into the modern world. It was seen by the poor and Indians as unmitigated land theft. It resulted in reducing the vast majority of Salvadorans to serfdom and the installation of a feudal economy over Salvadoran society. The Indians again rebelled but were crushed.

Peasant subservience to the landowner was assured through the efforts of local militias. Terror became the principal method of keeping workers from organizing. Landowners lent workers to each other as if bartering in slaves. This system functioned (at least in the eyes of the oligarchy) until 1932 when the rural Indian population in western El Salvador and workers in the capital rose against the landowners.

The military crushed this uprising, killing 30,000 Indians in the process. The Great Killing, as it is called, transformed the regional militias into a national institution and gave the military a key role in Salvadoran social life, a place it still holds today. Since the Great Killing of 1932 the military's main task has been to enforce the conditions that keep workers plentiful, unorganized and obedient to lawful authority, i.e. to the military themselves and to the landowners.

In the late 1970s the working classes of El Salvador again organized to demand higher wages and land reform. The landowners and military responded with the same, brutal efficiency that had characterized their repression of Indians in 1832, 1880 and 1932. In 1980 the United States, under the Reagan administration, replaced the Salvadoran oligarchy as the chief *patron* of the Salvadoran armed forces. With this exception, little has changed in El Salvador since the "liberal reforms" of the late nineteenth century that dissolved the communal lands. Finally, none of this will change as a result of the peace accord between the government of El Salvador and the FMLN.

A RATIONALE FOR WAR

This brings us back to Corral de Piedra. Why did the Salvadoran air force strike this small settlement with such ferocity on February 11, 1990? Why kill Jesuit priests, an archbishop, American nuns, and tens of thousands of civilians?

Corral de Piedra is an agricultural cooperative. A review of massacres and invasions over the past twelve years shows that cooperativists have been prime targets for attack by the Salvadoran armed forces. A cooperative is a self-sufficient, agro-economic model of development. Corral de Piedra is not a direct economic threat to the oligarchy. It subverts the economy, however, in that it is a model for economic self-sufficiency. A self-sufficient cooperative, even one that is very poor, does not provide labor for the annual harvest.

This helps account for the massacre of the Jesuits. Many in the Christian base communities, cooperatives and unions saw the Jesuits' deaths as an attack on economic and social self-sufficiency among the poor. The Jesuits still work openly and alongside the poor to undermine class dependency and institutionalized poverty. In this they are subversive of the economic status quo.

Oscar Romero was an economic subversive. He advocated programs, like land reform, that would have given the poor economic stability. A stable, economic base for El Salvador is contradictory to the interests of the landowners.

Archbishop Rivera Damas is a subversive. Under his leadership the social secretariat of the archdiocese has started a credit union program for small communities. Communities are given a small amount of capital to allow them to create a middle-interest account. They are allowed to keep this capital if the community invests. People who are saving money do not have to borrow at 20% interest to buy seed and fertilizer. If poor communities do not need the seasonal work in order to plant their staple crops, the export-crops would not be harvested.

Ironically, even capitalism is subversive to El Salvador's feudal economy. The oligarchy and military do not want to see an expanded middle class in El Salvador. Competition would force prices down and reduce the oligarchy's profit margin.

Until the conditions of dependency and institutionalized poverty change, the peace process and dialogue between the FMLN and the government of El Salvador means little. On the other hand, when cooperativists, like those from the Good Shepherd Agricultural Cooperative in Aguilares, can report that they are raising chickens and selling eggs on the open market without fear of reprisal from the large egg-producers, we will know that peace is coming to El Salvador.

When unions, like FENASTRAS, can organize and negotiate wages without their members being beheaded and their offices blown up, we will know that peace is coming to El Salvador.

When the archbishop of San Salvador, Arturo Rivera Damas, and Lutheran bishop Medardo Gomez can advocate the rights of the poor and marginalized without being called communists and threatened with death, we will know that peace is coming to El Salvador.

When free elections are held without ballots ending up in city sewers or "leftist" candidates killed, we will know that peace is coming to El Salvador.

News of a peace accord is a sign of hope. But El Salvador is a land of crushed hopes and there is ample cause for suspicion. The judge who heard the Jesuit case, Ricardo Zamora, apparently doubts the advent of peace with justice in El Salvador. After handing down his finding against a colonel and lieutenant, Judge Zamora announced plans for a lengthy sabbatical in Europe. "Flees the country" was the spin given to Zamora's decision by the *Washington Post.*

As the government and the FMLN were negotiating in New York, Mirtala Lopez, a courageous Salvadoran woman, who works with the Christian Committee for Displaced People of El Salvador, received five successive death threats from the Anti-Communist Society of El Salvador. These threats were accompanied by a candle dipped in blood and a five *colon* donation for a coffin. Shortly after, Mirtala came to the United States to speak about her experience. Despite the danger to her life she decided to return to El Salvador. Bishop Gumbleton of Detroit, Father Patrick McManamon of the Detroit Jesuit Province, Sister Alice Fairchild, a Dominican from New York, and two congressional aides—Hector Lucena (of Tom Foglieta's office, D-Pennsylvania) and Karen Masterson (of Tony Hall's office, D-Ohio) volunteered to accompany Mirtala to El Salvador. All were denied visas by the Salvadoran Minister of the Exterior. Mirtala Lopez has good reason to suspect whether justice is really coming to El Salvador.

Until we hear of changes at these levels, the New York Accord remains just another "message," "symbol," "indication of peace" and "sign," which like previous "messages," "symbols," "indications of peace" and "signs" may be a lie.

* * *

What will happen if the death squads become active again and the armed forces of El Salvador return to their total war mode of the early 1980s? This is possible, under any number of scenarios.

For example, the armed forces could easily manipulate the FMLN into an armed confrontation. The political space that has appeared in recent years in El Salvador is not the result of altruism on the part of the oligarchy and military. It grew, to a large extent, because of the sustained military effectiveness of the FMLN. For the FMLN to now agree to a cease-fire and enter the political struggle is a serious risk. The cease-fire made the front pages of the international newspapers. When the FMLN endorses candidates for elected office in El Salvador, this too will make news, although the back pages. But what would be the news value of the following succession of events: if the minister of the interior deports the international church workers and human rights advocates from El Salvador; if the government reneges on its agreed-upon reform of the armed forces; if the Anti-Communist Society acts on its promise to kill Mirtala Lopez; if selected leftist candidates meet with accidents?

El Salvador has already ceased to be news. Corral de Piedra did not make the news in the United States. The *New York Times* initially refused to carry the story of the Mozote massacre (800 killed). The Jesuit massacre had to compete for news-time with the effort to save two stranded whales in the Arctic. Renewed outbreaks of killing would receive very little attention in the United States, if any.

Yet the FMLN would respond to such attacks. Caches of arms buried in abandoned wells and grenades hidden in volcanic ravines would be retrieved. Some effort to organize would take place and a general call for an insurrection would be made. And there would be a great killing of the poor, the Christian base communities, unions and grass-roots, human rights groups.

A massacre of the poor could take place without help from the United States. The armed forces of El Salvador have not always relied on U.S. patronage. The state department may even object to the killing, but it certainly would not intervene to protect the poor. The important question is: How would the North American people respond?

INTERPRETING WAR AND PEACE THROUGH THE BLACK LEGEND

How North Americans would respond to a flare-up of violence directed against the poor in El Salvador would depend on how they interpret the information they receive. The dominant hermeneutic with which North Americans interpret news from Latin America is encoded in the Black Legend.

The term "Black Legend" was coined in 1912 by the Spanish historiographer Julian Juderias. It describes a four-centuries-old effort by England, Holland, France, Germany and later by the United States to morally discredit Spain and Latin America. The Black Legend is part of the conventional wisdom of North America:

—We learned how Spanish cruelty replaced Aztecan and Incan cruelty. Salvadoran death squads and torture, we think, make sense in such a context.

—We learned how the Spanish had conquistadors, the Incas and Aztecs their armies. Somehow these facts justify elaborate state security apparatus and armies in Latin American countries.

—We learned that neither the Spanish, with their inquisition, nor the Aztecs, with their human sacrifices, respected life. Massacres of students, peasants and workers by the armed forces of El Salvador appear quite "natural" to us in such a world.

—We learned how the Aztecs enslaved the Mayans and the Spanish enslaved the Aztecs. According to our conventional wisdom, Salvadorans have come to expect forced labor as a condition of life.

—We learned how Spanish viceroys replaced emperors and Incas. Hence, we do not expect to find any respect for democratic tradition in Latin America.

The Black Legend has not gone away. It has, however, acquired a sophisticated academic patina. One spokesman is Lawrence Harrison, a twenty year veteran of the Agency for International Development (AID) and writer on "underdevelopment" in Latin America. Harrison uses the sociological categories of Max Weber to account for violence and poverty in Latin America. According to Harrison, Latin America has failed to develop, not for lack of resources, nor because of foreign intervention, but for cultural reasons.

Harrison claims that the Spanish emphasis on individualism discourages "collective action and organization." Latin countries have no sense of *noblesse oblige*, he writes. Other ills of Hispanic culture that account for Latin American poverty and violence, according to Harrison: lack of trust, laziness, *machismo*, and authoritarian attitudes in child rearing (reinforced by Catholicism) that lead to state authoritarianism. All of these Spanish cultural qualities discourage the kind of liberal values Harrison posits are essential for development.

It is not enough to dismiss such conclusions simply because they mirror the Black Legend. (The argument holds, "Some stereotypes are true, even if they are disturbing.") These conclusions should be dismissed because they do not stand up to careful analysis and the record of history. The truth is that throughout Latin America, small but powerful cliques have kept the region underdeveloped for reasons of personal gain. El Salvador presents the clearest case:

—The oligarchy and military use violence to control the society. Violence is a means to an end, not a consequence of Spanish-Catholic culture.

—The oligarchy and military prevent economic cooperation

among the poor (cooperatives, unions, communal land movements). This reflects the avarice of the wealthy, not the individualism of the poor.

—The oligarchy and military undermine democracy. This reflects the oligarchy's unwillingness to share power, not the poor classes' lack of political interest.

All of this occurs with the collusion of the United States.

Harrison's work represents very old thinking about old problems. In attempting to dismiss "stale Marxist categories" like dependence and class conflict, he has repeated old clichés. It is true, as Harrison claims, that underdevelopment is a state of mind. But the state of mind that keeps Latin America underdeveloped and violent is the world-view of the Black Legend. This paradigm for interpreting Latin America has suppressed free thought and stifled development more than Spanish intolerance for dissent. As El Salvador enters into the post-Berlin wall era, it will become increasingly important to challenge the conventional wisdom of the Black Legend. It contributes to our indifference and makes us partners to oppression and the systematic subjugation of a hemisphere.

An earlier version of this chapter appeared in America, *Vol. 166, No. 1, January 1992.*

THE LIFE, SUFFERING AND DEATH OF
NELSON ALFREDO MOLINA
A Hermeneutic of Justice in El Salvador

On January 16, 1992 the leadership of the Farabundo Marti National Liberation Front signed a peace agreement with the Salvadoran government of Alfredo Cristiani. Many claimed that this peace accord was the "first negotiated revolution in history." If acted upon, it will bring about paradigmatic changes in Salvadoran society. Central to this accord is the dismantling of the military security apparatus and conversion of the police force to civilian control.

The events described here show the need to complete these parts of the Salvadoran peace accords. I chose to focus on a particular case, that involving Nelson Alfredo Molina, not for rhetorical reasons, but with the conviction that the tragic consequences of injustice are clearer when seen with a human face.

THE LIFE AND SUFFERING OF NELSON ALFREDO MOLINA

Nelson Alfredo Molina was eight years old in August of 1981 when the armed forces of El Salvador invaded his village, Big Rock Above, on the volcano of Chinchontepec.

Nelson's mother, Maria Catalina Molina, spotted the approaching soldiers while harvesting a fruit tree. Due to the absence of FMLN troops, Catalina may have assumed that the soldiers would bypass Big Rock Above. The soldiers also spotted Catalina. They bound her and began to lead her up the mountain. Nelson saw this from the doorway of his house and ran for his slingshot to protect his mother. He let loose a barrage of pebbles against the soldiers. The soldiers fired upon Nelson. Catalina screamed for him to get inside the house and Nelson retreated, frightened for his mother and terrified by the hate in the soldiers' eyes.

None but these soldiers witnessed the multiple rape-torture of Maria Catalina Molina. Nelson, his aunt Tomasa, and cousins found Catalina's body late that afternoon on a grassy knoll under a ceiba tree in the nearby village of Big Tree. The soldiers had punctured Catalina's body twenty-seven times using sharpened sticks and knives. They had cut off her lips and then taped over her mangled mouth to quiet her screams.

Tomasa placed her sister's body in the ground where she had been murdered. The family returned to their home, packed their few belongings and joined the long line of refugees seeking safety under the auspices of the International Red Cross in the nearby city of Zacatecoluca. In the confusion of their flight, Nelson became separated from his aunt and her family. Young and alone, the Red Cross officials sent Nelson to the refugee camp maintained by the Catholic archdiocese of San Salvador at San Jose Montana.

The refugee camp at San Jose Montana was a monotonous assembly of tin-roofed sheds constructed on the soccer field behind the archdiocesan seminary. The refugee population at San Jose swelled to over two thousand during late 1981 and early 1982. The refugees suffered depression, malnutrition and terrible disorientation. As one of the camp leaders described the first few months in the camp, "We had to decide whether to live or to die. We decided to live and that meant to continue the struggle." The refugees put their communal organizational skills to work and created a plethora of projects to better life in the camp: a clinic, a child-care program, schools and workshops. They formed committees for administration, sanitation, finances, correspondence and solidarity. Life did not return to normal but orderliness replaced the refugee's sense of alienation and *anomie.*

At San Jose Nelson developed a creative way of dealing with the painful memory of his mother's torture and death and his guilt for failing to protect her. He started to draw and to paint. When pencils, paper and paint became exhausted, Nelson continued to paint in his imagination. He created a catalogue of fantastic paintings that he could describe in exacting detail of tone, shape, content and color. Nelson told me ten years later that he painted these images in order to forget.

After six months Tomasa appeared at the refugee camp looking for Nelson. She and her family had fled to Guatemala and upon returning to El Salvador had established a squatter-house near the town of Apopa. Nelson joined Tomasa in Apopa. He accompanied his aunt to the market every day and sat by her side, running errands, carrying loads and continuing to create images in the refuge of his imagination.

As Nelson created, he continued to forget. His aunt replaced his mother. His cousins became his brothers and sisters. The creatures of Nelson's imagination became his friends. Fantastic scenes of volcanic slopes, bountiful harvests and sweet mountain streams took the place of market clutter, the clamor of streets and the accumulated smells of rotting garbage.

In early 1986 Tomasa learned of a project in nearby Calle Real to resettle people displaced by the war. She spoke to the pastoral team in Calle Real and was accepted as a candidate for the new community. The community was to be built on a garbage dump. The people formed a provisional government. They formed work teams. A communal dormitory and kitchen were established. Work proceeded in stages. The construction took a year to complete. At the end of the year the families celebrated with a mass of thanksgiving and drew lots during the offertory to choose their homes. After mass each family moved into its home to resume a normal life, the best that could be lived in the midst of war.

One month later an earthquake hit El Salvador and destroyed every home in the new community. The work of rebuilding began immediately.

Six months later the community was reconsecrated and people hoped for a modicum of peace.

But peace was not to be found in El Salvador in 1986-87. Calle Real is situated between the volcanoes of Guazapa and San Salvador. From the meeting house in Calle Real the people witnessed the nightly fire-bombing of Guazapa and the daily stream of refugees fleeing for the safety of the church. Calle Real mobilized to help the new refugees and displaced persons with the same creativity and spirit that had typified their time in the refugee camps.

Two of the women who had formed part of the health team in the refugee camp established a parish-based clinic. The former nursery school teacher started a kindergarten. The men began a collective garden. Four women formed a bakery. Another group started a seamstress cooperative. And the young men and women began planning a carpentry shop and arts collective—a place to learn and to earn and so help sustain their families.

Nelson joined the effort to build the carpentry cooperative. He made the small crosses and cedar boxes that other workshops purchased in order to paint with the popular folk-motifs of El Salvador.

As orders for the Calle Real crosses and cedar boxes increased, the carpenters decided to paint their own products, thus eliminating the middle-man and making a greater profit from their work.

Nelson had become a "conceptual artist" in his years since the refugee camp. He had the ideas but hadn't painted enough to master control over materials and composition. He was initially frustrated by his inability to transfer the creations of his imagination to the medium of tempera on wood. But he persevered and eventually his art began to show signs of promise.

Peace was announced in El Salvador on December 31, 1991. Nelson's liberation from a scarred past coincided with the unfolding of the peace. He fell in love with Mayra, a fifteen year old community health worker from the parish clinic. He continued to dream and to share his dreams with others. He painted more and his paintings began to resemble those of his imagination.

As he painted, Nelson also started to remember. During the first few months after the peace was announced, Nelson's memory was flooded with images of his mother. He did not see her tortured, raped body but rather remembered her face, smile, and sense of protective warmth. He recalled her many embraces and moments of childhood counsel. As he remembered, he painted. He continued to fall in love and announced that he intended to marry.

The return of memories did not invite rancor or a thirst for revenge in Nelson. He experienced some guilt in front of his aunt for distinguishing between her and his mother. But Tomasa proved wise and welcomed the new signs of outward life in her nephew. Nelson's suffering seemed to have passed without leaving any deep scars. He was alive and in love.

THE DEATH OF NELSON ALFREDO MOLINA

On March 5, 1992 Nelson left the carpentry shop at four in the afternoon and, after showering, went to the school in Calle Real for a rendezvous with Mayra. As they sat on the train tracks behind the school, four men approached and demanded that Nelson give them his shoes. These four were known to Nelson and Mayra as members of a drug-gang with reputed ties to the military. Their leader, Wilfredo Perez, was known to have killed before. Nelson surrendered his shoes.

Perez then demanded Nelson's glasses. Nelson refused. He

explained that his glasses were a prescription and that he needed them for his work as a carpenter and artist.

Two of the men dragged Nelson to his feet. A third, Reyes Guzmann, pulled back Nelson's head by the hair while Wilfredo Perez drove a knife into Nelson's heart, killing him instantly.

This all took place in front of Mayra who knew each man by name and where each lived. The killers made no effort to attack Mayra nor to threaten her. They simply retreated quietly after taking Nelson's glasses, shoes and wristwatch.

JUSTICE FOR NELSON ALFREDO MOLINA

Such tragedies occur with increased frequency in developed and undeveloped countries. Young men in Los Angeles, New York and Miami are killed daily for basketball shoes, sunglasses and wristwatches. True, Nelson's murder appears more tragic given this young man's life of suffering. Too often, however, we focus on the individual tragedy and fail to move to analysis. What merits attention in Nelson's case is not so much his death but the lack of interest in prosecuting his killers.

The next morning Mayra went to the national police headquarters in the municipality of Ciudad Delgado to report the crime. The police claimed that they could do nothing without an order to capture the killers from the first justice of the peace.

This was not true. Salvadoran criminal law allows the police to take a suspect into custody based on the testimony of a witness if testimony is given within twenty-four hours of the crime. Mayra went to the justice of the peace who escorted her back to the police and ordered them to accompany her to Calle Real and arrest the killers.

One of the killers, Reyes Guzmann, was apprehended sitting outside his house eating an apple. He didn't appear alarmed, only surprised to see the police. He was taken into custody. The time was now past five in the afternoon, however, and the police refused to return to Calle Real until the justice of the peace had completed his order to detain the other killers.

This order was completed the following day with testimony provided by Mayra, Tomasa and a cleaning lady at the school who had witnessed the two young people go to the tracks and Mayra's flight after Nelson's murder. The order to detain was then sent by the justice of the peace to the national police headquarters where it was lost.

Wilfredo Perez remained free. Members of his gang threatened to kill Mayra if she testified against Guzmann. They told Mayra that if they could not kill her they would seek their vengeance on her five year old brother, David.

Reports of sightings of the killers came to Calle Real. Tomasa continued to pressure the police to capture the killers. The police claimed that they were looking for Perez' gang.

The priest in Calle Real also pressed for justice. In one confrontation with the police captain, the captain blurted out that he was not looking for Wilfredo Perez and his accomplices because he had still not received an order to do so from the first justice of the peace. The priest gathered the witnesses once again and each renewed their testimony in front of the justice of the peace. This time the justice suggested taking a certified copy of the detention order to the national police headquarters in San Salvador and insisting that the *commandante* in the national office send an order to Ciudad Delgado to arrest the killers.

On April 12, 1992, the captain of the national police in Ciudad Delgado responded to this pressure from the Calle Real community by sending a squad of police to the church and bus stop below the church and arresting every young man from fourteen to twenty-five years old. The captives were not formally accused of any crime. Nor were they charged. They were held overnight in a crowded jail and each made to pay from thirty to seventy *colones to* be released.

The priest learned of the mass-arrest the following morning and accompanied mothers of the detained young men to the jail. He asked the captain why the police had chosen to capture the innocent and let the guilty go free. The captain looked bored with the question, but when the priest persisted he said: "Look, Father, nobody cares about this Molina case. I don't care. The justice of the peace doesn't care and the national police do not care. Nobody cares. You asked for more police presence in Calle Real and you now have it. These young men looked suspicious and so we took them in."

The priest asked why, if the youths were not to be formally charged, they still had to pay to be released. The explanation: due to the lack of resources in the justice system, the police needed money to purchase typing paper, carbon and other stationary supplies necessary to process the prisoners' release.

The bribes were paid and the young men were freed. As the priest left, the captain called him aside and said, "Be careful, Father. There's going to be more of this."

Repeated visits to the police proved equally vain. Two months after Nelson's death Wilfredo Perez killed again. This time his victim was an elderly woman on a public bus. After her family was visited by members of Perez' gang they decided not to press for police action.

In early June two of the killers appeared at a soccer club dance in Calle Real. Nelson's cousin, Esperanza Ayala, and her boyfriend, Francisco Geronimo, went to the police station to inform the detectives. Geronimo was himself a former national policeman and familiar with police procedure. He offered to pay the police to arrest the killers, veiling the bribe as an offer to pay for their taxi to Calle Real. But the police still refused to act and the killers remain free. Soon, Reyes Guzmann will be brought to trial. If Mayra is too scared to testify, he will be released.

A HERMENEUTIC OF JUSTICE

Wilfredo Perez does not have a political reputation. He is not known to harbor any rancor for the FMLN, cooperativists or organized communities of displaced people. From this point of view, Nelson's murder was not politically motivated. Why then, in the face of clear-cut evidence and the opportunity to capture Nelson's killers, have the police steadfastly refused to act? This is the hermeneutic question of Nelson's death.

The common response of the people, based on years of experience and suffering, is that Wilfredo Perez has "connections" to the armed forces of El Salvador. The claims are heard: "His uncle is a colonel in the air force," or "His cousin is a captain in the army," or "His brother is in the national guard." Such family connections serve to interpret crime in El Salvador. They make sense out of what would otherwise seem an incomprehensible lack of concern for murder on the part of the police.

Is the claim true? In many cases it is. In the case of Wilfredo Perez it is rumored but difficult to prove. Even if the family connection is true, this only explains why Perez acted without concern for the consequences. Perez had been arrested before and released. He has reason to believe that he can kill with impunity. But this does not explain the lack of police interest in the case from the start of the investigation.

Another hermeneutic to the inactivity of the police implicates the military and police in the activities of gangs, such as Perez'. There is increasing evidence surfacing in El Salvador linking high and middle military officials to the activities of drug gangs, smuggling operations, kidnaping for extortion, and protection rackets. Here again the general case holds, although evidence is not available in the particular case involving Nelson's murder.

Complicity of the police with criminals is not unique to El Salvador or to the third world. It is greatly facilitated in El Salvador, however, given the structure of the security forces, a structure that places the police under military command. As a consequence people are arrested (or not), tried, freed or released after trial based on the decisions of military personnel and not according to a uniform code of conduct. Law enforcement is arbitrary and depends largely on connections and access to the military.

The most comprehensive hermeneutic, or key, to unlocking the mystery of Nelson's murder was provided by Maria Julia Hernandez, the founder-director of Tutela Legal, the Catholic archdiocesan human rights office. When presented with the details of Nelson's case, Maria Julia Hernandez said that Tutela Legal could not lend an investigator to the parish in Calle Real precisely because cases such as Nelson's were occurring with great frequency across El Salvador. Investigators simply were not available. "This is important for you to understand," Maria Julia told the pastoral team from Calle Real who visited her office, "that as tragic as this young man's death was, it is typical. We have had five cases like this from Soyapango last week alone. More cases have been reported from Aguilares, Apopa, Ilopango and San Salvador. They all have the same characteristics: the victims are members of cooperatives or organized communities; the killers are known or there is strong evidence as to their identities; there is indifference on the part of the police."

She offered the following key to interpreting the state of justice in post-war El Salvador: The Salvadoran "security forces"—the national police, the national guard and the treasury police—are still under military control. They are loyal to military comrades and not to the constitution as interpreted by civilians. Critical to the peace agreement is the dismantling of these security forces: the complete elimination of the national guard and treasury police and the transformation of the national police into a civilian controlled, national civil police.

At the time of my interview with Maria Julia Hernandez, the national guard had simply changed its name to the frontier police and transferred three thousand members to the national police. The treasury police had changed its name to the national military police, a move that places this security force closer to the military high command. The national police were waiting to be re-formed under civilian control.

Maria Julia explained that across El Salvador, the national police had moved into the forts formerly occupied by the national guard to assume responsibility for public security. But once in place they have resolutely refused to act in cases of violence directed against organized communities, cooperatives and displaced people's organizations—all considered as facades for the FMLN by the military.

Maria Julia Hernandez' conclusion: the national police are fomenting civil unrest by not prosecuting clear cases of crime against organized communities. This inaction is intended to undermine people's efforts to organize communities, unions and cooperatives. It is intended to create a general state of terror leading to an acclaim for the return of the military security forces.

The consequences of Nelson's death were felt in Calle Real in ways that support Maria Julia Hernandez' thesis. The members of the parish-based cooperatives became apprehensive of meeting. The health workers stopped visiting communities. The pastoral team in Calle Real considered suspending its effort to pressure the police to arrest Perez.

But there was no acclaim heard in Calle Real for the return of the military security forces.

CONCLUSION

There are, undoubtedly, many and conflicting reasons why the Salvadoran national police have refused to enforce the criminal code and ignore the constitution of El Salvador. Maria Julia Hernandez' interpretation links police inactivity to police self-interest. Her hermeneutic makes sense.

In law enforcement, not to act is to act in collaboration with the criminal. The police officer stands for law. When the police observe crime without acting or fail to prosecute criminals they are interpreting the law through *praxis*. People are quick to see the patterns and note what law is, in its ideal sense, and what law really is in El Salvador.

If Calle Real is a window to the Salvadoran reality, the Salvadoran air has been cleared of the euphoria of peace. The people have come to realize that peace is not created by signing a piece of paper. Peace demands justice. A society without a process for defining right and wrong, and without the means of enforcing these norms, will never know peace. According to Maria Julia Hernandez, this lesson has been learned in numerous communities with losses equal to and in some instances greater than Calle Real's.

As a consequence, Salvadorans are focusing a great deal of attention on the demilitarization of their security forces and the incorporation of new candidates into the promised civilian police.

This interest on the part of the Salvadoran people challenges the international community. While control of the security forces remains in the hands of the military, justice will remain but a dream in El Salvador. The necessary changes have been outlined in the peace agreement. They must be acted upon. Until that happens, to support the present system is to support state terror and murder.

THE CHURCH AND THE "NEW POPULAR ECONOMY"
Problems and Prospects

The "new popular economy" is an effort to restructure economic relations within and between Salvadoran communities in a way that gives the poor access to raw materials, control over the means of production and direct access to markets. It further allows them, through their own labor, to support social services in their communities. The Catholic archdiocese of San Salvador has emerged as a major promoter of the new popular economy. A case in point is the parish of Calle Real, eight kilometers north of the capital of San Salvador.

The health project in Calle Real served 16,500 people in 1991. The range of medical needs addressed by the health team was varied. About one-third of the patients who visited the clinic were suffering from common colds, grippe and fevers that required little more than a sympathetic ear and a dose of aspirin. Other patients were treated for intestinal diseases, bronchitis, skin infections and more serious illnesses. The diagnoses were made by promoters of health—lay persons trained by the archdiocesan commission on pastoral health. More complicated cases were seen by a doctor or medical student.

From 1987 until 1992 the archdiocese of San Salvador provided the clinic in Calle Real with an annual subsidy of 27,000 *colones* for the purchase of medicines. The promoters of health "sold" this medicine to their patients for 9,000 *colones* and used this income to maintain the clinic facility. In 1992 the archdiocese announced that after January 1993 the clinic in Calle Real would no longer receive this subsidy.

The nursery school-kindergarten in Calle Real cares for fifty children. Each family contributes one *colon* per day to the nursery school. This covers one-third of the costs of materials, salaries, and food for the children. The other two-thirds of the costs have been provided by a one-time, non-renewable gift from Catholic Charities in Spain. In 1993 these funds will expire.

The Mothers and Infants Program provides a dietary supplement to one hundred and fifty families, mostly single-parent homes living as squatters along the rail tracks in Calle Real. The Mothers and Infants Program has been administered for thirty years by Catholic Charities with surplus foods donated by the U.S. Agency for International Development (A.I.D.). In December 1992 Archbishop Rivera Damas requested that a portion of administrative funds for this project be allocated for job-training in squatter communities. A.I.D. refused the archbishop's request. Consequently, in late 1992 the Mothers and Infants Program will be eliminated, the victim of A.I.D. intransigence.

In short, in 1993 the three major assistance programs in Calle Real will be without funding. Literally thousands of men, women and children will be affected. The consequences in El Salvador, which does not provide social services to the poor, can be catastrophic.

The clinic, nursery school-kindergarten and Mothers and Infants Program are part of the "Cooperative of the Social Pastoral of Calle Real," a collective that also includes five "productive" cooperatives: a bakery, a seamstress shop, a carpentry shop, an agricultural credit union and a construction workers cooperative. The long-range vision of the Cooperative of the Social Pastoral of Calle Real is to sustain social services with the work of the productive cooperatives. Only in this way will the cycle of poverty, which is nourished by dependence, be broken.

INTEGRAL HUMAN DEVELOPMENT

The criterion for the social pastoral of Calle Real is taken from the social teachings of the Catholic Church, particularly the pastoral letters of San Salvador's archbishop Arturo Rivera Damas. Archbishop Rivera Damas has spoken clearly and forcefully on the right of all sectors of society for "integral development." For Rivera Damas, "integral development" is the most basic human right, one that provides a foundation for all other rights—civil and religious. Integral development does not prioritize food and shelter over psychological health and spiritual well-being. It does not regard work as more important than cultural-artistic expression. It sees all of these as essential for human development and stresses them all.

For Rivera Damas, a program that provides food to the poor but robs the poor of their dignity does not contribute to human development. A program that provides work but does so sacrificing the right of workers to organize does not advance human integrity. A development program that replaces God with the false god of history is counter-development. Every activity proposed by or supported with funds of the social secretariat of the archdiocese attends to the integral development of the program's beneficiaries: their physical well-being, psychological health, spiritual growth and cultural advancement.

Given El Salvador's repressive social structure and the internalization of repression by the culture-at-large, the archdiocesan pastoral plan is a revolutionary manifesto. It calls for profound changes in Salvadoran society, the evangelization of structures and the personal conversion of the faithful. Changing governmental and economic structures without changing the persons who create and maintain these systems is a waste of time, or so says the Catholic Church in El Salvador.

Attention to "integral development" prompted the pastoral team in Calle Real to review and revise the social service projects described above. An example:

The goal of the clinic in Calle Real is to provide the best quality service to the poor by reducing costs, especially profit, of health care. It is not a professional, full-service hospital. Costs are reduced by the presence of volunteer health promoters. They are reduced by the not-for-profit distribution of medicines. Medicinal costs have been further reduced by developing natural medicines for the pharmacy. Patients who are able also help reduce costs by cleaning the clinic facility and watering the plants. Some patients provide plants to the medicinal garden.

The most difficult attitude to convey to the clinic's patients is that the facility is their responsibility to maintain. These are not seen as typical or professional approaches to health care. But a popular clinic does not reflect popular values simply because filing, laboratory analysis, consulting and preventative work are done by peasants. It is a popular clinic when it is maintained financially and through contributed labor by the people who use it. To pay for maintenance, support services and commercial medicines with subsidies received from outside the parish would increase dependence and so be contrary to integral development.

Integral development means more than providing health care. It includes giving the sick the opportunity to become healers. Clients of the clinic in Calle Real are instructed in preventative health, about the use of herbs as curatives, the nature of their illness and how to become well. Just as importantly, they are asked to contribute to the health of others by becoming involved as health promoters. This may involve cleaning the clinic or a more serious commitment such as becoming involved in the works of diagnoses, education, laboratory analysis or pharmacology. This is integral development for health: becoming cured and curing others.

JOB TRAINING FOR SELF-SUFFICIENCY

The pastoral team realized in 1986 that the social services it provided would never be completely self-sufficient. There exist national and international agencies which support health and child care in the third world. But the Calle Real team realized that to create programs dependent on this kind of outside assistance would be counter-productive. It would not encourage responsible partnership on the part of the needy and would make the pastoral team, which lacks direct access to international agencies, dependent upon fund-raising agencies, each of which has a political agenda.

Rather than increase dependence, the pastoral team in Calle Real decided to improve the quality of life in the community through job-training. The hope was that by increasing the community's standard of living, the community would eventually be able to sustain the social services of the church. Consequently, in 1986 the pastoral team started a carpentry shop, a seamstress shop and a bakery. Each of these projects eventually failed, victims of two forces.

To maintain a training workshop requires continual income for teachers' salaries and raw material for the students. Calle Real lacked these resources. The products initially made by the students were not marketable. Furniture fell apart. Clothing was poorly designed, cut and sewn. Worst of all, the bakery developed a reputation for making *pan piedra,* "stone-bread." The bakery provides a case in point of a misguided job-training project. The small group of women working in this bakery received inadequate technical training. They received no training in accounting or economic theory. Common sense dictated that people would not purchase bread if basic ingredients were eliminated, like yeast. But when confronted with their initial slow sales, and the need to feed their families, they started to steal money reserved for raw materials. The quality of the bread worsened. On numerous occasions they went to the nuns in the parish for loans. The nun who administered the parish assumed control over their accounts. When she was present in the parish, the bakers could get funds. When she was not, they had to make bread without certain ingredients.

This did not improve the situation. Rather than skimming money for raw materials, the bakers skimmed the materials themselves. In addition to worsening the condition of the bread, the bakers never learned how to manage their accounts. The bakery closed.

The lay members of the pastoral team eventually saw a more profound problem inherent in the training-approach to economic development. They asked, "What advantages are we gaining for the majority by educating a few to incorporate into a work force that is itself oppressive?"

The oppression of the Salvadoran workers is legend. They are underpaid. They are seldom paid social security, and when social security is paid it is as a reward for loyalty to the *patron* and not for work well done. Workers are divided. Their unions are constantly attacked by the government and union leaders killed by death squads. Some unions are controlled by political forces more loyal to Marxism than to their workers. Preparing laborers to enter such a work-force is hardly a sign of integral development.

In 1989 the archdiocese of San Salvador announced a mission to "evangelize the structures of Salvadoran society." The Calle Real pastoral team interpreted this as a challenge to envision new forms and relations of work, not to simply train workers to enter a repressed work force. The pastoral team developed a plan to place control over the means of production in the hands of the workers.

The plan that emerged challenged the dominant ideology of the ARENA Party which neatly divides the world between "producers" (those with capital) and "users" (those with the capital to purchase what the producers make). This ideology fails to recognize the existence of "workers" and their dual role as producers and consumers. The Calle Real pastoral team dreamed of creating a multi-service, multi-product cooperative, legally incorporated, with the capacity to export, and with control over all aspects of supply, production and market. The social pastoral of Calle Real was subsequently reorganized into two arms: projects of assistance and projects of production. The team looked for economic assistance for five years to provide training and help to build an economic infrastructure. The goal was that in five years the cooperatives of Calle Real would be able to sustain the social services in their community through a tax placed on the profits of the cooperatives.

THE WORKER AS PRODUCER AND CONSUMER:
A REVOLUTION IN CONSCIOUSNESS

The first project to become reorganized in Calle Real under this new structure was the carpentry shop. Moved to a new location and with a new shop made available with assistance from the Jesuit Faith and Justice Center in Toronto, Canada and the Loyola Foundation in Washington, D.C., the Loyola Carpentry Cooperative began operating on February 11, 1990. The first two years were devoted to learning technical skills and producing furniture appropriate to the technical levels achieved by the carpenters. The start-up grant from the Jesuit Faith and Justice Center paid the original salary for the teacher. After a year, the carpenters paid the teacher's salary from their earnings. In 1992 three of the young carpenters from the Loyola Cooperative became teachers.

At first the carpenters earned very little and made no profit. They gradually opened markets, and by time of this writing, August 1992, have twenty-two young people producing in three areas: housing construction, furniture making and folk arts. Salaries are increasing monthly and some profits beyond salaries are beginning to show.

In 1991 the Cooperative of the Social Pastoral of Calle Real received a great boost through the generosity of a small foundation working in El Salvador. The Salvadoran Humanitarian Assistance, Research and Education (SHARE) Foundation responded favorably to Calle Real's request for sixty thousand dollars to build a clinic and pastoral center. The pastoral team indicated in its request that the carpentry cooperative would produce all the furniture for the center. Iron work would be sub-contracted to another church-based cooperative. The cement blocks would likewise be purchased from another cooperative. Finally, the greatest cost—labor—would be performed by a construction workers' cooperative formed for that purpose. The proposal stipulated that the construction cooperative would continue to function after construction was completed. The grant application stipulated that 10% of the overall costs would be paid "up front" to the new construction cooperative to purchase machinery and tools.

The SHARE Foundation deserves a great deal of credit for its part in the birth of this cooperative and the construction of the center in Calle Real. The proposal they received was bold and imaginative, but nothing in the history of the parish indicated that the pastoral team had the ability to accomplish the goals set forth in the proposal. SHARE took a risk, more impressed by imagination than by the technical and fiscal preparedness of the Calle Real parish. In fact, SHARE went further and linked Calle Real with a parish in Louisville, Kentucky, the Church of the Epiphany, which continues to support the development of a new popular economy in Calle Real.

The construction workers and carpenters built the pastoral center of Calle Real in four months. It was blessed by Archbishop Arturo Rivera Damas on August 16, 1991 during the parish corn festival. The construction workers had little time to rest. They went on to build a school in Paisnal and another in Aguilares, both for poor communities at a considerable savings to these communities.

The clinic moved into its new locale. Other spaces in the pastoral center were occupied by the construction workers, a new bakery (the Resurrection Bakery) and a revitalized seamstress cooperative. Each of these projects, along with a credit union started in 1992, is helping to sustain social services in Calle Real.

PROBLEMS IN THE NEW POPULAR ECONOMY

The story of the growth of cooperativism in Calle Real is encouraging. These advances, however, have been won with just as many setbacks. The Calle Real experience suggests that bringing about a new, popular economy requires overcoming three major hurdles. These are: creating new structures of social relations within work, developing an appropriate methodology for administration and accountability, and securing funding for training and infrastructure.

NEW STRUCTURES OF WORK

The need to develop new structures of work can be illustrated with an example from the construction industry. In El Salvador, a client who wants to build contracts a construction firm. They agree on a plan and price and the client makes a thirty percent down-payment. The construction firm provides technical oversight and places a master of works over the project. The master of works' first task is to hire the laborers. That done, he oversees the construction until the owner takes possession of the building.

There are four classes of laborers on a Salvadoran construction site. First, the master of works hires laborers to work directly under him. These are paid twenty-eight *colones* ($3.50) daily. Some are paid social security. Second, the master also hires qualified laborers, for example, bricklayers, to execute the skilled work on a pay-as-you-build basis. Bricklayers are paid one *colon* per cement block. A bricklayer may lay one hundred cement blocks in a single day, but from the one hundred *colones,* he must pay his helpers who mix mortar and deliver blocks to the bricklayer's designated portion of the construction site. These assistants are the third type of laborer on a job site. They are paid less than the general laborers. They are not paid social security. Finally, at times the master of works hires day laborers through a "coyote." In this scheme he earns a kickback by cheating the laborers. Instead of hiring ten laborers for ten positions at twenty-eight *colones* per day, he sells these ten positions to the "coyote." The coyote looks for day laborers to fill these positions and pays them one half the minimum wage, fourteen *colones* daily. He and the master of works then split the difference, gaining seven colones each for each laborer, solely because they control who works and who does not work.

As a result, laborers on a Salvadoran construction site are constantly competing with one another. The laborers compete for access to building materials. The bricklayers compete to lay more bricks in a limited space of time. There is competition between "qualified" and "unqualified" laborers. Day laborers earning fourteen *colones* per day resent the contract laborers who earn twenty-eight *colones.* Such competition is contrary to the interests of the workers who never have a unified forum to negotiate with the owners of the company. They are structurally divided before the work ever begins. This structure is also contrary to the interests of the client who wants the building well-constructed. If the bricklayers are paid for the number of bricks laid, and not according to their time, they hurry and the quality of construction lags. In earthquake-prone El Salvador this has dire consequences. Walls that are not exactly plumb will cave in after the first few earthquake trembles.

When the construction workers' cooperative started in Calle Real, the workers immediately organized themselves according to the norms described above. Members of the pastoral team were astounded by this. The laborers of the coop were the owners of the means of production, not simply workers. As owners, their interests should have been toward making a greater profit for the cooperative. This required showing an interest in all aspects of production and not simply performing a limited role. Yet, despite a high degree of political consciousness and an intellectual commitment to cooperativism, these workers had never experienced work other than in the mode of the dominant society. Making the transition to a cooperative structure was extremely difficult. It required more than a critique of the existing structures of work. What was needed was an internal conversion on the part of each laborer toward working in a cooperative.

Such a conversion also requires a different style of social communication. In a typical Salvadoran work site, all laborers work under the master, who in turn works under the owner of the contracting firm. In the construction cooperative of Calle Real, the workers are the owners. The master of works—also a member of the cooperative—works for the laborers. The workers needed to learn how to follow the directions of the master without surrendering authority over cooperative governance to him. Issues of governance—participation in administrative decisions, planning and training—ultimately belong to the associates of the cooperative, not to the master of works.

ADMINISTRATION OF A POPULAR ECONOMY

Competent administration delineates areas of expertise and authority so as to decrease costs, improve production and open markets. The first problem in creating competent administration for the new popular economy is that the typical Salvadoran worker lacks a wide perspective on a functioning economy. In most circumstances the Salvadoran worker never sees administration taking place. The Salvadoran worker simply follows orders without understanding the whole process of supply, production and marketing. The Salvadoran laborer regards the boss as the culmination of all power in a social system where power is arbitrary.

Another cultural characteristic of the Salvadoran worker that discourages efficient administration is the tendency to emphasize personal relations over work roles. Indeed, lacking an understanding of administration and the differentiation of work roles, they collapse work roles into personal roles, which they do understand. In the traditional Salvadoran system, the boss is also the patron who takes care of the worker and the worker's family. A typical attitude toward worker-welfare is that the government need not supply social security to the worker because this is the responsibility of the patron. It is a great irony to see how, in many rural communities, poor families seek out the most abusive (yet powerful) patrons and landowners to be godparents for their children. This is an attempt to personalize work roles and to transform the boss into a member of the family.

The need to develop administrative roles and the difficulty in doing so is evident in the brief history of the seamstress shop in Calle Real. This cooperative started as one of the parish training workshops. The sewing teacher, Narci, was initially paid by the parish. When funds ended she offered to "help" the cooperative by bringing their embroidery work to market. Narci evolved into the *patron* for the seamstresses. The women did not know where Narci sold their work or for what price. They remained ignorant of costs and market demand. They simply worked and received a pittance every month from Narci, whose revolutionary rhetoric was never matched by her deeds.

The social pastoral team eventually insisted that at least one other seamstress become familiar with Narci's marketing outlets and sources of raw materials. Narci then resigned. Another woman, Demetia, was elected to take Narci's place. Just as Narci had duplicated the traditional role of *patron*, so Demetia duplicated Narci's roles as well.

There was one exception. Demetia is an honest woman and she did not steal from her colleagues. She located new markets and profits increased as did salaries. Orders for work streamed into the shop. The women designed new products and located new sources for raw materials. Profits increased and additional women joined the cooperative. After six months it became clear that the administration of the shop needed to diversify outside of Demetia's control. The pastoral team mandated that the cooperative elect a president, secretary, treasurer and disciplinarian.

The elections were duly held, and, according to most observers, the newly-elected officials were exactly the worst for each position. Demetia returned as work coordinator. The president-elect, a hard worker and honest woman, was painfully shy and had no ability to preside over a meeting. The secretary could not write. The treasurer could not add or subtract. The disciplinarian was the youngest member of the cooperative and the person most needing disciplining.

What had happened? Confronted with a mandate to elect administrators to complement Demetia's role as work coordinator, the members of the cooperative chose to accede in a way that would not threaten Demetia. Ironically, all agreed on the need for a new style of administration. But until Demetia herself was ready for that change, the decision was not to force it and hurt her feelings. The personal relationship was more important than the role-relationship.

The problem facing the creation of a new, popular economy is to respect the accent on the personal while developing roles that will see tasks accomplished.

FUNDING FOR TRAINING AND INFRASTRUCTURE

All reconstruction funds for El Salvador channeled through the Salvadoran government are designated for the support of the existing economic infrastructure. For example, the government has received funds for retraining ex-combatants and returned refugees. But agencies collaborating with the government will only train men and women to enter the private sector. It will not train men and women who wish to work in cooperatives. Cooperativism challenges the alliance of large industry and the Salvadoran government. The United States government regards cooperativism as a soft form of socialism. The department of state of the United States, which has made training funds available through A.I.D., supports the Salvadoran government's lack of support for cooperatives.

Popular organizations and non-governmental organizations (NGOs) in El Salvador have also raised money for reconstruction and training. These funds are small, in comparison to those received by the government from A.I.D. More problematic, many NGOs have a top-down approach to development. Although espousing revolutionary rhetoric that calls for the empowerment of the "masses," they manage funds and projects for the poor, assuming the role of *patron* left vacant by the former *patrons*. Top-down development does not work. It is particularly ineffective when the rhetoric raises the workers' expectations for greater participation in economic decision-making, but the reality reduces the workers to passive cogs in the machinery of a neo-socialist economy.

With such small amounts of funds reaching Salvadoran communities and cooperatives, there is little prospect for building a strong base for a new popular economy in El Salvador.

This leaves the churches as the main source of channeling funds to the communities. The Lutheran Church of El Salvador was once a major participant in the new popular economy. But the Lutheran Church's close alignment with the communist party has weakened the integrity of the church and lost it support in the international community. Some Baptist churches and the Episcopal Church of El Salvador have maintained their integrity and promoted a new economic reality in El Salvador, but with extremely limited material and human resources.

The Catholic Church shows the greatest potential to contribute toward the creation of a new economic structure for El Salvador. The social secretariat of the archdiocese of San Salvador has supported placing economic production in the hands of Salvadoran workers. The church has a clearly articulated social program, one based on a long tradition of social doctrine. It has maintained fidelity to this doctrine and not sacrificed its integrity for political expediency with the FMLN nor compromised its social vision for an opportunity to become co-administrator with the United States Agency for International Development of reconstruction funds.

The Catholic Church's difficulties in assuming a major role in reconstruction stem from its lack of personnel and its inability to interact with international funding agencies and potential corporate donors.

The church's lack of support-personnel is most evident in the communities where there are not resources to teach the poor simple accounting and management practices. The list is long of communities robbed by hired professionals or "popular organizations" interested more in the resources the communities attract than in the works they set out to accomplish. Qualified personnel are also lacking to improve social communication skills within projects. Without such skills, peasants and laborers fail to develop active roles in their communities and cooperatives. They then become prone to political manipulation.

The inability of the church to interact with international funding agencies and corporate donors is partly a consequence of the lack of personnel. It is also the result of the church's xenophobia and inability to delegate authority. Here again, the social secretariat has reason to maintain a healthy suspicion of foreigners and political manipulation within its ranks by the FMLN. The church's reaction to this possibility, however, has limited its ability to secure funding for poor communities.

CONCLUSION

Salvadoran workers and peasants waged a twelve year struggle to gain the political advantages now emerging under the watchful eyes of the United Nations and the international community. If Salvadoran workers and peasants cannot refocus their incredible energy and creativity to wage an economic offensive, their struggle will have been fought for nothing and the advantages gained will prove to be temporary. These workers and peasants need to transform the economic reality of El Salvador on all levels of society. Their offensive must include gaining access to the sources of raw materials for industry, production and marketing of products—in short, the creation of a new popular economy.

The church's role in this process of social transformation is important but limited. The church's role ends with providing models for a new society, as is emerging in Calle Real, and helping these communities develop the infrastructure needed to become self-sufficient. The greater task of creating a more just national economy properly belongs to secular agencies, albeit with the moral counsel of the church. The Catholic archdiocese of San Salvador is playing its role as teacher and prophet. The final transformation will come about in El Salvador, however, when the Salvadoran masses call all of the social institutions in that country, including the FMLN, to greater accountability.

EL SALVADOR'S HARVEST OF JUSTICE
Confession, Reconciliation, Conversion

As El Salvador heralded 1992 as the "year of peace," and Archbishop Rivera Damas called for national reconciliation, it became evident that, before reaping their harvest of justice, Salvadorans would have to acknowledge the storm that racked their society for twelve years. Even families that had suffered losses during the war at first hesitated to admit that the suffering and oppression were as widespread as they indeed were. This is not difficult to understand. Denial is one way to manage stress, especially when the causes are beyond the individual's control. But El Salvador cannot begin the process of healing until the wounds of war are acknowledged, people are allowed to publicly grieve, and society and individuals commit to change.

El Salvador's eye on the past is personified by Maria Julia Hernandez and her crew of investigators from the archdiocesan human rights office, Tutela Legal. Soon after the signing of the peace accord in Mexico City, Tutela Legal began journeying to El Mozote, the Sumpul River, Copapayo, San Sebastian and countless other sites of horrible massacres of defenseless men, women and children to search for evidence as to what happened. These cases and nearly one thousand others were presented to a National Commission of Truth in mid-August 1992.

The majority of cases placed before the National Commission of Truth document atrocities committed by the armed forces of El Salvador against defenseless civilians—some alleged supporters of the FMLN. The motives for these atrocities were pragmatic. The defenseless were killed—precisely because they were defenseless—to instill terror among the survivors. The terrorized are malleable and easier to govern.

The FMLN, while generally not guilty of huge massacres, was also guilty of human rights abuses and has acknowledged many of these. Sometimes it executed within its own ranks—as in the case of

Roque Dalton. It sometimes assassinated mayors, members of military families and political supporters of the right. The FMLN must also answer for its crimes, make a public commitment to change, and be held accountable to that commitment.

More than the armed forces of El Salvador and its supporters, and the FMLN and its supporters, will have to answer for crimes against humanity committed in El Salvador. The citizens who chose to remain ignorant, or, when confronted with the truth, chose to remain silent, will have to answer for their part in this national tragedy. The people of the United States will have to answer for their complicity, and particularly those officials who misled congress and used the Salvadoran insurrection to fan the flames of anti-communism. If lasting peace is to come to El Salvador all of these parties must commit themselves to change.

This essay treats of two instances of reconciliation in this wrenching moment of the Salvadoran tragedy, one unresolved, the other in the process of resolution. The first case is typical—involving the denial of wrong on the part of the United States government. The second is atypical. It involves the part played by an FMLN combatant in the execution of suspected infiltrators.

UNITED STATES POLICY TOWARD EL SALVADOR: WEAKNESS AND DECEIT

The extensive killing of innocent men, women and children by the armed forces of El Salvador has been documented by journalists, human rights monitors, neutral governments, church workers and the survivors themselves. It would require an elaborate conspiracy indeed to bring these many voices into harmonic synchrony, as one voice condemning the Salvadoran government and armed forces for twelve years of murder. Missing from the list of the valiant who denounced injustice are the names of United States Embassy personnel, any of the men who occupied the Latin American desk at the United States department of state, and presidents of the United States during the Salvadoran insurrection.

Silence in the face of injustice may be construed as complicity. Worse, representatives of the United States government lied to the American people, to the congress of the United States and to the world, claiming that the violations had not occurred, the dead had not died, the suffering only imagined their suffering. Worse yet, the

United States government actively fueled the Salvadoran killing machine with over four billion dollars in aid during the twelve year war.

The claims of journalists, human rights organizations and churches created a problem for the Reagan-Bush administrations. The U.S. Foreign Assistance Act of 1961 says that "no security assistance may be provided to any country which engages in a consistent pattern of gross violations of internationally recognized human rights." President Reagan and his appointees in the department of state were required by congress to certify improving human rights in El Salvador as a prerequisite for continued assistance. These certifications and the mandatory Congressional hearings have left a record of shameful denial and a lost opportunity to provide American foreign policy with some moral legacy.

Thomas Enders was assistant secretary of state for inter-American affairs in the early years of the Reagan administration. Enders had earned the trust of the right-wing of the Republican Party for his cover-up of Cambodian atrocities. (Enders once hailed General Lon Nol's fraudulent election as "a step forward for Cambodian democracy.") Ignoring the massacres that took place in 1980 at the Sumpul River (600 killed) and San Pablo Tacachico (31 killed) and in 1981 at Guazapa (34 killed) and Armenia (23 killed), Enders testified before congress on September 24, 1981 that "the level of violence has apparently decreased over recent months, we believe, in part due to the government's efforts to end the abuses that have occurred in (El Salvador)."

Enders' greatest test of credibility came in late December 1981 and January 1982 after the massacre at El Mozote. The El Mozote massacre was horrible and senseless: horrible because of the extent and kind of suffering; senseless because, even by Salvadoran military standards, it didn't terrify the population. It left all dead and none left to terrify. The Mozote massacre was part of a ten day operation led by Domingo Monterrosa. According to *New York Times* correspondent Ray Bonner, "the first column of soldiers arrived on foot in Mozote at about 6:00 A.M. More soldiers were landed by helicopter. The villagers were ordered out of their houses, into the tiny square in front of the church, men in one group, women in another. The men were blindfolded, taken away in small groups of four or five, and shot. Women were raped. Of the 482 Mozote victims, 280 were children under fourteen years old."

The total number of victims eventually reached 1,200, the majority women and children. The day after the story of the massacre appeared in the *Washington Post,* President Reagan certified to congress that the Salvadoran government was making "a concerted and significant effort to comply with internationally recognized human rights." Enders added his voice, claiming that "there is no evidence to confirm that government forces systematically massacred civilians in the operations zone, or that the number of civilians even remotely approached the 733 or 926 victims cited in the press."

The killing continued into 1982, 1983 and 1984. The state department continued to deny that the killings took place or that the U.S.-trained special battalions participated in these. The pattern of death and denial continued throughout the war, into the final months of 1991.

Why this twelve year pattern of "weakness and deceit," as Bonner has characterized U.S. policy in El Salvador? By most standards El Salvador is strategically unimportant to the military and economic interests of the United States. What did Thomas Enders, the Connecticut patrician, find so threatening in the illiterate and poor peasants of Mozote?

The answer cited during the decade of the 1980s was the threat to world stability posed by a possible Soviet foothold in Central America. But the Soviet Union was disintegrating from its own inner corruption as the United States was propping up the Salvadoran government and military. More likely, El Salvador had become a symbol of resistance, and symbols are sometimes more threatening to the status quo than peasant armies.

When peace was announced, El Salvador slipped from the front pages of U.S. newspapers. A few journalists monitoring the peace process wrote articles about the demobilization of guerrilla forces. Then articles appeared (now on the back pages) concerning the promised contribution of the Agency for International Development (A.I.D.) toward reconstruction. Although this aid was being promised in 1992, in the midst of a terrible recession, it was not uncommon to hear people comment that "I don't mind the government sending money to El Salvador. God knows those people deserve it." Not exactly an acknowledgement of guilt, but at least an admission that the people of El Salvador merit help. I suggest that this support is more important for Americans than Salvadorans, constituting a kind of subjective absolution. The American sentiment seems to be: "We know some awful things were done. We are sorry and now we'd like to help."

The questions North Americans failed to ask about foreign aid during the war must be asked now. Will A.I.D.'s contribution help El Salvador? Will it encourage reconciliation, or aggravate class tensions? Will foreign aid help make the Salvadoran economy autonomous, or increase dependence upon the United States? Will foreign aid reach those who need it most, or contribute to their oppression?

In April 1992 the Regional Program of Investigation on El Salvador (PREIS) presented preliminary results of their study on the United States Agency for International Development's influence on El Salvador during the decade of the 1980s. The results are not encouraging, particularly given A.I.D.'s role as a principal partner in Salvadoran reconstruction. No aid is better than some kinds of aid, particularly the kind of aid promised by A.I.D.

This claim needs to be placed in context. There are three economic models competing in El Salvador. A.I.D. supports one of these. These three are: private-ownership of business, state-ownership and worker-ownership. The first model has the support of the ARENA Party and A.I.D. The second has little support in El Salvador, except among die-hard socialists. The third has the support of the vast majority of peasants and workers, and is not recognized by A.I.D. Yet, worker-owned cooperatives are recognized under the constitution of El Salvador. They have their own tax-structure. They give the workers an active role in industrial management.

In worker-owned cooperatives, control remains in the hands of the active work force. This form of private ownership protects the workers from outside manipulation by persons with greater capital resources. Worker-owned cooperatives are socialist in some aspects but accountable to market forces. Most importantly, they do not contribute to centralization of the economy. If productivity declines, so does profit. They receive no government support for inefficient management and so do not contribute to inflation.

According to PREIS, the private sector has been the principal beneficiary of A.I.D. assistance in El Salvador. A case in point: AID has made available retraining money for ex-combatants and returned refugees. This is laudable. However, A.I.D. norms will not allow worker-owned cooperatives to participate in this training. Only workers who are going to work for the "private sector" as individual laborers can receive the training. Cooperatives must pay for the retraining of ex-combatants and displaced people. This places the cooperatives at an unfair disadvantage when competing with the "private sector." Ironically, A.I.D. support for the "private sector" has developed as a form of welfare for the rich and has made private industry less responsive to market forces.

Another influence of A.I.D. in El Salvador is its support for "privatization." Here again it is important not to interpret privatization in El Salvador with the template of North American political categories. The government of El Salvador provides few social services to its people. It receives foreign grants to build public clinics and then fails to staff them. Public education provides little more than day care. Electrification, potable water, garbage removal and much road construction is either provided with foreign assistance or through non-binding community initiatives. The few social services the government does provide, the governing ARENA Party wants to privatize. And it is doing so with A.I.D.'s assistance.

Those who can pay will educate their children. Those with money will receive health care. Communities that are legally incorporated will be able to secure and maintain electricity, water and sanitation. But for the poor who lack resources, these facilities will remain beyond the pale.

Reconciliation is important to El Salvador. One way of socially instituting reconciliation is through representative government. The United States government's practice of promising aid and then making it contingent upon political considerations undermines representative government. This political manipulation was evident in post-Sandinista Nicaragua. In the interest of fostering national reconciliation, the Chammorro government opted to leave the Sandinistas in charge of the ministry of defense. With the collapse of the Soviet Union, Nicaragua posed no threat to American interests. But Nicaragua was to become, once again, a convenient political prize tossed to the conservative wing of the Republican Party. According to Senator Jesse Helms, until Chammorro removed the Sandinistas from government, promised American aid would be withheld.

Will A.I.D. support for reconstruction in El Salvador be contingent upon Salvadoran acquiescence to the vagaries of American politics? Whatever happens in El Salvador after the 1994 elections, we can be sure of one thing. The political complexion of El Salvador is going to change. Some municipalities will elect FMLN mayors. The constituent assembly will almost certainly include former guerrillas, some communists, Marxists, Leninists, and other assorted radicals. Indeed, some analysts speculate that the FMLN could gain control over the assembly. The FMLN will expect and deserve some role in government. El Salvador needs reconciliation. In the political camp this is best achieved through support for democracy and representative government. El Salvador's powerful hemispheric neighbor must reconcile itself to the fact that Salvadorans know better than Jesse Helms how to achieve national reconciliation. If this means support for cooperativism, so be it. If it means FMLN control over certain ministries, so be it. If it means public regulation of industry, governmental support for the arts and environmental standards for all, so be it. If A.I.D. continues to undermine democracies, invoking the dubious slogans of private initiative, privatization of social services, and individual freedoms, Salvadorans will never enjoy the harvest of justice so many have struggled so long to reap.

A FAITH BEST RESERVED FOR GOD ALONE: CHURCH AND GOD IN THE SALVADORAN REVOLUTION

There occurred in El Salvador another violation of human rights—this one committed by the FMLN—that raises a disturbing question in light of national reconciliation: how to remain faithful to the struggle when human institutions fail that trust. I present this case, corroborated by numerous witnesses and families of the victims, as a commentary on the nature of faith when faith is misdirected away from God and toward a social institution, like the FMLN.

For two months in 1986 and again in late 1989 the FMLN leadership on the volcano of San Vicente investigated its squads operating on the volcano in order to uncover a suspected infiltrator. The evidence of an infiltrator was strong: ambushes, rear attacks and interrupted supply and courier lines. As a result of these investigations, one hundred and ninety FMLN combatants were executed, some after terrible interrogation-torture. Eventually the infiltrator was identified: the captain who had led the investigation and ordered the executions. He was a deep plant of the Salvadoran armed forces within the guerrilla ranks. Along with other collaborators he was responsible for these deaths as well as those of the guerrillas killed in ambush.

The captain's motives were clear. He killed to eliminate his enemy. He killed in a very effective manner.

The FMLN leadership allowed the captain to kill because they wished to locate the infiltrator, not realizing that the infiltrator was the captain himself. The strategic decision was apparently made by the FMLN that the security of the San Vicente stronghold was more valuable than the lives of loyal troops. The historical goal required the sacrifice of individuals.

How was this possible, not for the captain to kill, but for his men to allow him to kill? I offer the following testimony as a key to understanding this question. The speaker is Julio, a sixty year old former combatant from San Vicente. Julio's three sons and two daughters were also combatants. Julio's wife was a courier between San Salvador and San Vicente.

* * *

When the investigation began, I was assigned to lead the suspects from a small corral, up the mountainside to the place where the captain was conducting the interrogation. Sometimes the men and women in this corral were guarded; most often they were not. So loyal were we to the revolutionary struggle, so faithful to our cause and so ready to sacrifice for it, that we did not consider that the suspects might run away.

I can't forget what took place. I recall leading a comrade, Pedro Mendoza, up the hillside and leaving him with the captain and the other interrogators. I left for the second suspect and returned, as ordered, after an hour. Pedro was hanging upside down from a tree. He'd been beaten. Many of his bones had been broken but he was still alive. The captain ordered me to cut Pedro down and to remove him to a common grave.

The new suspect—the one I had just escorted—offered to help me. But first he said to the captain, "My captain, I am innocent. But I submit myself to this interrogation and will go to my death because I know that you must locate the enemy. I just want you to know that, whatever I say under interrogation, I am innocent."

He helped me to drag Pedro's body to a grave site. I cut Pedro's neck with a machete and we buried him. I would have let this other suspect go, but he returned with me to meet his death. And so it went all day for two weeks on end.

On October 7, 1986 I myself was ordered to report for interrogation. I was told that my outside contacts had made me suspect. I resigned myself to my fate and reported to the waiting area.

There were no guards that day, only the man who had assumed my job of leading the suspects to the execution site.

I waited and the first suspect was taken to his death.

The guard returned and escorted the second suspect to his death. I waited.

The guard returned and escorted the third suspect to his death. Each time the guard returned more bloodied. I waited.

The guard returned and said, "You know what they are going to do, friend."

"Yes," I said. "But I'm innocent."

"I believe you, but that doesn't matter. Your fate is sealed. Do you know why they suspect you?"

"Because of my outside contacts, they said."

"Do you know who these suspected outside contacts are?"

"No," I responded.

"Your wife. She is a courier. The captain says that you are the infiltrator and your wife is the courier. When she next appears here, she'll be interrogated and killed.

"Listen," he said, "your wife led my family to safety in 1982. I know that she is innocent. I don't want to be part of her death, or yours.

"I have to piss. When I return I'll have to escort you to your interrogation."

* * *

Julio didn't wait. He took his friend's cue and left for San Salvador where he intercepted his wife before she left for San Vicente. He arrived in San Salvador on October 10, 1986 at noon. A half hour later an earthquake struck San Salvador. In the confusion created by this disaster, Julio and his family were able to disappear. They have remained loyal to the FMLN and have recently become active helping the FMLN to organize as a political party.

Two of Julio's sons died in the war—combatants for the FMLN. "My greatest fear when I learned of their deaths was that my sons had died while being interrogated and not fighting the enemy. During my grieving I realized that I had come to believe in the FMLN as if it were God and incapable of making mistakes. When I learned of the death of my sons, and imagined that they had been killed by the FMLN, I realized that some faith is best reserved for God alone. I could believe in the justice of our cause and dedicate myself to the struggle. I could suspend my personal judgment and surrender my life in obedience to the FMLN, but it was wrong to give the FMLN this faith that belongs to God alone. I had witnessed the evil of the enemy. I had also witnessed the dedication and goodness of my companions. And I had still led them to their deaths as I myself had been willing to be led. This was wrong."

How did Julio come to place such faith in the FMLN? He and his family were not devoutly religious. They were Holy Week Catholics who participated in the popular cult of the church as a cultural activity and not as an expression of faith. Their faith in God was awakened by a priest working in San Vicente in the late 1970s.

This priest, David Rodriguez, initially worked with the young people in the small cantons and villages of San Vicente. He was a guitar player, singer, story-teller, and a man deeply in love with the scriptures. He formed youth groups as a way of sharing this love with the young men and women of San Vicente and Chinchontepec. He taught them to see their own lives within the word of God. He taught them to look for solutions to their problems in scripture.

Eventually more than the youth of San Vicente came to experience a renewal of faith. Julio began to study the Bible. "I couldn't read, but I could listen," Julio explained. "At first I felt that I had nothing to offer, but Father David encouraged me and soon I was offering my opinions and experiences to the study group." Julio came to see the struggle of his own people in the struggle of God's poor. He came to believe that God sided with the poor and was committed to their struggle. Through the study of scripture, the practice of the sacraments and the study of the traditions of the church, Julio, his family and community came alive in their faith.

They began organizing activities in their canton as a response to this faith. They built two chapels that also served as schools. They planted community gardens and organized themselves to negotiate with the landowners in their district. It was then that their activities met with swift retaliation from the national guard and the private armies of the landowners.

After the first wave of disappearances, killings and captures, the people went to the bishop of San Vicente for help. "We did not ask Bishop Aparicio to agree with the demands we had placed before the landowners. We simply wanted him to speak for our right to organize." Not only did Aparicio not support the people, he publicly condemned them. When some men occupied Aparicio's cathedral, he ordered the national guard to retake it by force. The protesters were captured, tortured and their body parts strewn around San Vicente. Among these was Julio's brother-in-law.

"We should have learned from this, but we did not," Julio later reflected. "Some of us left the movement; others left the church. It was David Rodriguez who cautioned us that our faith was in God and in the struggle of the poor, not in the church. Those of us who remained active in the struggle needed to understand this distinction. The church is a human institution, imperfect and at times corrupt. Only God is perfect.

"But we didn't really learn. We maintained our faith in God but simply transferred our faith in the church to the revolutionary organization. At the time this seemed reasonable. The facts were these: all efforts to secure our rights through peaceful means had failed. The armed struggle seemed our only option. When my two sons joined the newly formed Militia for Popular Liberation, we knew that this decision affected the whole family. If they were captured, killed or identified we would all suffer. My sons' commitment required complete unity. There could be no room for individual options in the historical struggle for the community. The individual and individual rights would have to be suspended for the sake of the historical struggle."

For Julio and many like him, his faith in a God of history was replaced by a faith in God as history. Political instructors replaced catechists. Talk of history replaced God-talk. Historical necessity replaced moral necessity. The revolutionary leaders understood the strength that faith brought to the struggle. They sought not so much to displace religion as to control it.

Julio is not a passive man. He was a guerrilla leader with the rank of lieutenant. He had killed to defend himself and his community. Yet, when ordered up the mountain to face certain torture-death, Julio was obedient to the FMLN. He knew he was innocent and yet was willing to be led to his death for crimes he had not committed because of his belief in history as God. Julio told me that his wife's visits had kept him sane during the invasions, massacres and life in guerrilla camps. He was willing to die for her in the revolutionary struggle, but not willing to let the revolution kill her. His love proved stronger than his faith, and that love saved Julio and his wife.

What challenge does reconciliation present to Julio?

He must reconcile himself to those who participated in untold massacres, invasions and killings. He must reconcile himself with the thousands more who stood passively by as these injustices were carried out. He must reconcile himself to the FMLN which sometimes abused his trust. Most profoundly, Julio must reconcile himself to God.

Julio has begun this difficult journey and has emerged as a

leader in his new community. Whether in the forums of the church, community or FMLN he offers thoughtful criticism and careful counsel, and he demonstrates an openness to the opinions of others. He has matured. He regards the FMLN as political parties should be regarded—human devices with internal contradictions and competing interests. He is supportive of the FMLN but critical. He is concerned about the lack of dialogue between the FMLN leadership and the people. He is concerned with the military structure of the FMLN and its need to develop a more open and democratic style. But Julio remains committed to the FMLN as the most viable political option for the poor in El Salvador and the struggle of the poor as one blessed by God. As Julio continues to reconcile himself to the new El Salvador, his contribution to the church and FMLN grows in richness. Julio's greatest fear is that the church and FMLN will be unwilling to accept him as a caring, thinking adult—faithful to God alone.

THE HARVEST OF JUSTICE

Before it can feed its people, secure its place in the world, provide for internal security and external defense and end the fifty year cycles of violence that have racked its society since 1832, El Salvador must accomplish the accords agreed upon in principle in New York on December 31, 1991 and signed in Mexico on January 16, 1992. Only then will the poor be able to reap the harvest of justice that they deserve.

The church has assumed a leading role in bringing about this harvest. Archbishop Rivera Damas is a member of the commission overseeing the implementation of the peace accords. *Tutela Legal* has presented careful evidence to the Ad Hoc Commission for the Purgation of the Armed Forces and to the Commission of Truth. The Social Secretariat of the archdiocese is participating in the creation of a new, popular economy at the community level. Every parish in El Salvador has hosted forty hours of prayer for peace, thus invoking popular religious practice and testimony to focus attention on the war and to motivate the people to commit themselves to work for peace. The church has remained prophetic in the face of El Salvador's changing political landscape. It has done so without becoming sectarian. It has challenged the FMLN and government to respect the poor, to support democratic initiative and projects that will benefit the majority and not simply the political faithful.

As Archbishop Rivera Damas has said in countless homilies, press interviews and speeches, El Salvador must change. This change must be societal and personal. Julio exemplifies the best possible scenario for Salvadorans. He has confessed his guilt as a collaborator in the death of Pedro Mendoza. As a result of this confession, Julio has earned the right to challenge the FMLN to greater accountability. He is no less committed to the struggle for justice, nor to the FMLN as a political force within El Salvador. But his relationship to the struggle and to the FMLN is different as a result of his confession, reconciliation and conversion.

The United States has not changed its attitude and policies toward El Salvador. The world that President Reagan evoked to justify U.S. policy toward El Salvador during the decade of the 1980s has certainly changed. But state department policies, and particularly the policies of A.I.D., have not followed suit. Nor has the United States abandoned the practice of allowing small, strategically unimportant countries like El Salvador and Nicaragua from becoming political footballs for right wing demagogues.

North Americans should follow Julio's lead. They need to acknowledge guilt and undergo conversion. Only then will El Salvador reap its harvest of justice. Until that occurs, the power of A.I.D. and the capriciousness of North American politics looms on El Salvador's horizon like a threatening storm.

TALKING ABOUT THE PEACE IN
EL SALVADOR
January 16–August 6, 1992

The rumors of peace had circulated since November. Some thought peace would be announced on Christmas Eve. When the good news failed to materialize, many reverted to skepticism. Others held out for the new year.

The radio announced the news at about nine in the evening on December 31, 1991. After twelve years of war, seventy-five thousand deaths, millions of exiles, refugees and persons displaced by the war, the FMLN leadership, the government and the armed forces of El Salvador finally came to an agreement on demobilization of their respective forces and the social-political changes required to allow the participation of the FMLN in elections. On December 31 the details of the accord were still sketchy. The promise was that on January 16 the two sides would formally sign an agreement in Mexico. Before the announcer could end his story and the commentators begin theirs, rural communities, city barrios, guerrilla encampments and many cooperative and union offices where people were listening burst into applause. In Calle Real the nuns opened the church and the altar boys and girls began ringing the bells, continuing until the new year arrived two and one half hours later—1992, the year of reconciliation and peace in El Salvador.

JANUARY 16, 1992:
THE PEACE ACCORD IS SIGNED IN MEXICO CITY

On the day of the signing many popular organizations supportive of the FMLN and the government of El Salvador sponsored an all-night festival in two adjacent plazas in downtown San Salvador. The government festival—with beer, numerous musical stages and festive banners—was held in *Parque Libertad*. The popular organizations staged their *fete* in the plaza in front of the Metropolitan Cathedral.

The caravan of buses, trucks, cars and wagons carrying people to this festival passed the parish of Calle Real at about ten in the morning. It came out of the north transporting thousands of unarmed FMLN combatants, their supporters, and members of communities and cooperatives. These vehicles were adorned with banners proclaiming "We have won the peace," "Here comes the *Frente*," "The final victory of peace," and other such statements. As the caravan passed on the highway below, the people of Calle Real—displaced by invasion, ravaged by twelve years of war and oppressed by militarization—waved their support and cried tears of relief:

Adela, the nursery school teacher, tears streaming down her face: "I never thought we'd see this."

Laura, the health promoter, all smiles: "At last, peace."

Antonia, the nun, earnest and sincere: "The people deserve peace."

Felipe, the Jesuit seminarian, eager to begin rebuilding: "Now we can work."

The faith communities of Calle Real celebrated a eucharist of thanksgiving and then loaded into their own mini-caravan of banner-draped vehicles destined for the celebrations. They parked on the edge of downtown and passed through the government-sponsored festivities in *Parque Libertad*. The crowd had still not gathered for the government-sponsored celebration, although the red, white and blue buses of the ARENA Party were beginning to discharge passengers into the plaza.

The cathedral plaza, on the other hand, was bursting with revelers by the time the Calle Real folks arrived in the late afternoon. A folk-music group was singing the popular anthem "The Blue Sombrero" on a large center stage. A chain of dancers, hundreds of persons long, was winding its way through the plaza, and on side-stages various speakers were telling stories of the war, reciting epic poems of "the struggle" and leading the crowd in traditional revolutionary songs. Vendors were scattered throughout the crowd hawking everything from soda pop to T-shirts with an FMLN logo blazoned across their backs.

Nighttime fell and the crowd grew larger. Crossing the plaza I stopped to gaze at the huge banners hanging from the front of the cathedral. All of these were pro-FMLN and none were subtle. As I stood there I happened to notice Julio also staring starry-eyed at the cathedral. I hadn't seen Julio for some months and was delighted that his cooperative had taken the effort to drive in from Cuscatlan. We greeted one another and I asked him what he thought about the peace.

"It's bitter-sweet," he said. "When I last saw my son he had come to tell me that he'd been transferred to Cabanas. We spoke a little, and when it was time to part, he said, 'Poppy, we'll be together again when there is peace. We'll meet in front of the cathedral, for the celebration of the final victory.' Well," Julio sighed, "I'm here but my son is not."

I noticed as many tears in the plaza that night as smiles. Everybody had lost some relative, friend or neighbor in the war. The people couldn't express their joy at the peace without it evoking memories of those who had sacrificed their lives to achieve it.

I continued my walk across the plaza, looking for friends from the San Miguel cooperative in Aguilares. I finally spotted their truck— a gaudy blue and white Ford—and sat down to talk over the peace. Here too there were smiles as well as tears. I sought out a friend, William, and we talked of peace. "Thank God and thank the FMLN for the peace," William said. "This really is a victory. It makes sense out of all that we have suffered and sacrificed."

But William was the first to hint that the peace also meant new problems for the poor of El Salvador. "My fear is that we are not ready," William said. Knowing his story and what he had suffered in the war, I asked what preparations were required by peace.

"Before the war we were little more than slaves for the landowners. The war changed that for some of us. It has given us confidence we never had before. When we were displaced from the plantations, forced to resettle in refugee camps and then leave to form our cooperatives and communities, we were able to rely on this new confidence. But we also had immense help from internationals. Peace means independence for the poor. The world will soon forget El Salvador. If the peace accords are followed, and I think they will be, we need to prove our ability to manage our agriculture, industry and government. I regret the time squandered and the opportunities lost when we could have learned more. I hope we are ready for the peace."

FEBRUARY 1, 1992: THE FMLN LEADERSHIP RETURNS TO EL SALVADOR

The exhilaration did not diminish in the first weeks following the signing of the peace accord. Talk of peace still rang of "victory," "achievement" and "jubilation." The skepticism of November had been dissipated by the realization that, if acted upon, the peace accords would amount to a "negotiated revolution," so sweeping were they in scope and consequence. There was another festive gathering in front of the cathedral on February 1, 1992, this time to welcome back to El Salvador the five *commandantes* of the FMLN. Once again caravans from the north, south, east and west converged on San Salvador. The crowds were jubilant. The plaza was crowded. One difference stood out from the January 16 celebration. The cathedral was not bedecked in FMLN banners, even though the celebration was ostensibly for the FMLN leadership. Instead, one banner graced the cathedral facade, that of slain Archbishop Oscar Arnulfo Romero. The slogan was simply put: "Monseñor, you have been resurrected in your people."

There was more dancing, speech-making, poetry and singing. There also appeared the first signs of fissures in FMLN unity. Despite the effort to stage all political events on the central stage and reserve the side stages for entertainment, the National Resistance—one of the five groups of the FMLN—insisted on presenting their own program on the side. I asked a friend who had been on the planning committee for the festival why this had occurred. "The unity we experienced in the war was born from need more than conviction. With the peace, some believe that there is no longer the need for unity. Or worse, they believe that unity is the other group changing its position to become more like their own. This is not true. If we learned anything during the war it should have been that unity is achieved through listening and compromise. This fracturing is the great affliction of the left. The war did not kill us," she said, "but the peace might."

The FMLN leaders visited their troops throughout February. As mandated by the peace accord they directed their troops to concentrate first in fifty and later in fifteen camps. This United Nations-supervised concentration of forces created yet another pretext for festivity. Communities far and near journeyed to the FMLN camps for weekend dances and other festivals. Peace-talk stayed optimistic.

MARCH 24, 1992: ANNIVERSARY OF THE DEATH OF OSCAR ARNULFO ROMERO

In late February and early March it became evident that the much-hailed guardian of the peace, the United Nations Observation Team in El Salvador (UNOSAL), was more devoted to observation than implementation of the peace accords. The peace process required that the guerrillas concentrate their forces in fifteen positions. Yet, no provisions for support services (food, shelter, re-education) had been made to sustain these camps. The UNOSAL chief in El Salvador made it very clear that this was not his problem. Faced with hunger and the imminent rainy season there was talk that the FMLN might return to its wartime positions, thus heralding a violation of the peace accord.

Only to make matters worse, the armed forces of El Salvador dragged its feet on implementing its part of the agreed-upon disengagement of forces. UNOSAL ignored FMLN protests and the situation rapidly deteriorated. The government apparently interpreted this as complicity and introduced some unique interpretations of the peace accords. They changed the names of the national guard and treasury police to the frontier police and military police, respectively, thus claiming to have disbanded both organizations. Military planes buzzed guerrilla camps, contrary to the agreed-upon disengagement of forces. Soon peace talk was replaced by talk of war from both sides.

But the peace had created an ambience of openness in El Salvador that had not been felt for decades. This ambience had two effects, both of which kept hope alive and brought out huge crowds on the twelfth anniversary of Oscar Romero's death. People had exposed their sympathies in the two months since peace was announced and there was now no denying loyalties. "We have to make this peace work," many members of base communities, popular organizations and churches said. "We've exposed ourselves. If we go back to war, we're all dead." Peace was now talked about as a task and not a realized objective. Slogans appeared on the walls of San Salvador's main avenues inviting all Salvadorans to "continue the struggle for peace." Even conservative businesses, eager to exploit the market possibilities of peace, joined in peace talk. The ultra-conservative National Association of Private Enterprise (ANEP) issued a challenge to unions to "maintain the peace." ANEP's understanding of peace was clearly different than that of the unions, but it too had come to see the peace not as an accomplishment but as an objective, now closer at hand, but still unachieved.

More profoundly, the people of El Salvador had hungered for the freedom that comes with peace, and, once tasted, were not willing to slip into war once again. During the Romero anniversary celebration, the people did not speak of peace as a victory, but rather as "work," "commitment" and "struggle." The naive optimism of January was replaced by the mature realization that peace-making was a life-struggle. Speakers from the popular organizations, communities and churches prayed for peace, but, more importantly, they prayed for the strength to make peace happen. Archbishop Rivera Damas admonished both sides to continue to dialogue, and his voice was joined by many in the international community. The FMLN and the government responded, and shortly afterward, the peace process was back on track.

AUGUST 6, 1992: FEAST OF THE SAVIOR OF THE WORLD

By May and June the demobilization of FMLN forces, while delayed, was back on a regular cycle. Talk of peace in El Salvador was clearly spoken of now as a project. Rosario Acosta, the leader of the Center for Field-Workers, a popular organization representing thousands of poor, landless peasants, gave an interview where she linked peace with economic justice. "Peace is not a signed document," Rosario said. "It's the fruit of labor made possible by economic justice." She warned the membership of the CTC: "Peace demands a commitment to organize, a dedication to struggle and continued faith in the creation of a just society."

Fortunately, in their fervor to dedicate themselves to peace-building, most Salvadorans have developed a mature assessment of the FMLN and the popular organizations. Rosario Acosta has spoken of the necessity for "the struggle for peace to take place within the popular organizations." "We cannot build peace on passivity," she has said. "Peace means all of our members having an active voice in decision-making and then dedicating themselves to the wishes of the people. You can't build peace on blind faith. Peace requires intelligence."

The associates in the San Miguel cooperative now speak of peace as the product of labor. William, the peasant who had earlier expressed concern for the readiness of his community for the peace, spoke in early August of the "need for economic resources to develop self-sufficiency. Then we will see peace in El Salvador." William's remarks were delivered at the dedication of a school in the cooperative. His concern, and that of his fellow associates, was for the quality of education for the young and how they would support the school. "Peace is the product of labor," William said at this inauguration, "and the labor of peasants requires land. If we are going to build peace in El Salvador, the landless poor need access to land. How is that different than 1977?"

On August 6, 1992, during a mass celebrating the feast of the Savior of the World, El Salvador's national feast day, Julio Quinonez spoke of peace to his new community in the Department of Cuscatlan, on the volcano of Guazapa. The occasion was a peace vigil organized by the local pastoral team. The congregation that assembled in this parish church was mixed. Some, like Julio, were ex-combatants of the FMLN. Others were ex-combatants of the armed forces of El Salvador. Many had spent the war in blissful ignorance.

"We are here to celebrate peace," Julio said. "And I've been asked to say something about that. I have fought in two wars—the 1969 war with Honduras and in the recent struggle. I lost two of my sons in the last war. I don't mind telling you, they were part of the forces of liberation.

"I never want to lose another son to war. If you want peace, say no to war. No more war. Never again. No war."

A tear formed in the corner of Julio's eye. He brushed it away and apologized to the congregation for not being a very profound public speaker. "When I say no to war, I say no, not only to the generals and *commandantes*. When it gets to that point, it's too late. We must say no to the war fought in the home, to the war waged against the worker, to the war waged against women and against the poor. Peace means saying no to every injustice, no matter how small or how large. Do not let the small injustices grow into large injustices. Say no to all war and say yes to life."

REMAINING VIGILANT

The night before I left El Salvador I visited my friend, Maria Luisa Lopez, and her Christian base community on the volcano of San Vicente. I parked my truck in front of Maria Luisa's adobe house, and at four in the afternoon we left for the meeting that was to take place further up the volcano. We arrived at the community center at five, cleaned the floor and wiped off the benches. When the first people arrived, Maria Luisa initiated a singing practice. Our voices carried over the trees and hills, announcing to the nearby households that the meeting was about to begin.

A small table had been placed in the center of the community house. By the time the community had gathered, this table sagged under the weight of tamales, jugs of coffee, tortillas, cookies and sandwiches. At 6 P.M. Maria Luisa offered the prayer and began the meeting. After the prayer and another gathering song, Maria Luisa signaled her granddaughter to begin the celebration of the word.

Cradling the Bible in her hands, this young girl began to read the Lukan passage where Jesus commissions his disciples, sending them out in pairs to spread the good news. She didn't read well, although her voice was clear and she projected it with strength. Her reverence for the Bible in her hands more than compensated for the lack of dramatic delivery. I had heard this passage read on many different occasions. But that evening on San Vicente I understood it in a special way. I wanted to go forth and announce the reign of God as I had seen it lived in El Salvador.

The people of El Salvador have not been blessed with an innate wisdom giving them special insights into the reign of God. Ironically, their blessing is their curse. Because they have been cursed with a terrible suffering, they understand more readily and respond to the word of God directed toward the suffering poor of history. That places the people of El Salvador, and particularly the faith communities, more squarely in the tradition of the *anawim*.

189

Theirs is a tradition of exile and promise to return, the experience of hundreds of thousands of Salvadorans;

A tradition of prophets, like Oscar Romero, Ignacio Ellacuria and Maria Luisa Lopez;

A tradition of community, as is lived in countless parishes, cooperatives and Christian base communities;

A tradition of martyrs, the reality of the church of El Salvador and its 75,000 dead.

El Salvador is proof that the church grows strong in adversity. It triumphs because of difficulty. The blood of its martyrs makes fertile barren ground.

El Salvador's tradition of suffering has been punctuated by moments of rebellion and resistance. The Salvadoran peasants recognized from the start that the so-called "liberal reforms" of the 1800s were no more than a legalization of land theft. The Indian leader, Anastasio Aquino, organized a rebellion in the 1830s to resist this enslavement. Aquino and his movement were crushed.

Farabundo Marti organized a similar national resistance one hundred years later. This movement was similarly crushed and followed by a great massacre of Indians, peasants and unionists.

Fifty years later, in the late 1970s, Salvadorans again organized themselves to resist the overwhelming power of the oligarchy and military. They did this by entering the political arena. When the elections were stolen, the resistance took the form of popular protest, often receiving the support of the church. Demonstrators were killed, organizers tortured and their supporters jailed and driven into exile. As an act of desperation, remnants of the political and popular resistance formed a unified military structure, the FMLN. In 1992 the government of El Salvador negotiated a peace accord with the FMLN. The peace accord paves the way for full democratic elections in El Salvador in 1994.

Three conditions differ today (1992) than in 1832 when Aquino led his rebellion and 1932 when Farabundo Marti organized the peasants and workers to resist the oligarchy.

First, when the Salvadoran church identified itself as a "church of the poor," the struggle of the poor became transformed into a faith struggle. The impulse for change in El Salvador is not simply a reaction to injustice (as was Aquino's rebellion) nor a response to injustice guided by a Marxist analysis. It springs, rather, from the very soul of the Salvadoran people.

Second, as part of its contribution to the struggle for justice, the churches and popular organizations have established organizations to document and report violations of human rights. Tutela Legal of the archdiocese of San Salvador, smaller diocesan commissions of human rights, the Lutheran Church's *Soccoro Legal*, the Non-Governmental Human Rights Commission, and the Institute for Human Rights at the Jesuit University are attentive to the changes taking place in El Salvador and quick to publicize violations of the peace agreement.

Third, the eyes of the world have become focused on tiny El Salvador. The efforts of the Salvadoran organizations struggling for peace have been joined by international agencies such as Amnesty International, America's Watch, the Washington Office on Latin America, the European Economic Community and the United Nations. People are paying attention to these organizations and responding to violations of human rights with political and economic pressure. Many church communities, North American religious leaders, academics, politicians and labor leaders have visited El Salvador and have heard first-hand of the suffering of the Salvadoran people and of their valiant efforts to resist oppression. This accompaniment seriously curtails the oligarchy and the military's ability to move against the poor. But this brake on violence and state terror depends upon continued vigilance.

Finally, another change has occurred between the time of this writing (1992) and the 1980 outbreak of resistance and rebellion in El Salvador. The international balance of power between the United States and the Soviet Union has completely changed. United States support for the Salvadoran military was based on Jeanne Kirkpatrick's famous logic that it is better to support an authoritarian regime (as she understands quasi-democracies like El Salvador) than a totalitarian one (a Marxist state). But with the crumbling of the Berlin wall and the advent of improved U.S.-Soviet relations, the United States can no longer justify support for Salvadoran authoritarianism with reference to Russian totalitarianism.

The frustration felt by many North Americans who learn about El Salvador is expressed by the cry, "But what can I do?" First, it is important to remain vigilant. Only if we maintain our watchfulness can we help foster peaceful change in El Salvador. We can do this by exerting influence on Congress, responding to boycotts of Salvadoran agribusiness. We can contribute materially to the reconstruction of a society that our tax dollars has helped to destroy. We can support solidarity groups working directly with Christian base communities in El Salvador.

Or we can do nothing.

* * *

After the meeting of the base community on San Vicente, I accompanied Maria Luisa Lopez back to her home. I visited with her family. We drank coffee and told stories. My friends marveled that by that time the next day I would be thousands of miles away from them.

I slept well that night and woke at dawn. Before getting into my truck and leaving for the airport, we tarried, avoiding the moment we knew would be so painful for all of us. Finally, I stood to embrace each member of Maria Luisa's family, saving the most difficult farewell for last. Maria Luisa walked me to the bed-spring door of her family's compound. As we stepped into the street she asked me: "Will you remember me?"

"Of course," I said, feeling a little hurt that she should ask this.

"And will you tell people what you've seen here?"

"Yes," I insisted. "You know that I will."

"And what will your people do?" she asked. "What will they do?"

RECOMMENDED READING

Books

The Promised Land, by Jenny Pearce. Published in Great Britain by the Latin America Bureau, distributed in the United States by The Monthly Review.

Don Lito of El Salvador, by María López Vigil. Orbis Books, Maryknoll, New York.

El Salvador: A Spring Whose Waters Never Run Dry. Edited by Scott Wright, et al. EPICA Press, 1470 Irving St, NW, Washington, DC 20010.

Religious Roots of Rebellion, by Philip Berryman. Orbis Books, Maryknoll, New York.

War Against the Poor: Low-Intensity Conflict and the Christian Faith, by Jack Nelson-Pallmeyer. Orbis Books, Maryknoll, New York.

Salvador Witness: The Life and Calling of Jean Donovan, by Ana Carrigan. Ballantine Books, New York.

Condoning the Killing: Ten Years of Massacres in El Salvador, by the staffs of the Ecumenical Program on Central America and the Caribbean and the Commission for the Defense of Human Rights in Central America. EPICA Press, 1470 Irving St, NW, Washington, DC 20010.

Death and Life in Morazan: Testimony from a War Zone, by Rogelio Ponseel. CIIR Publications. Distributed in the United States by EPICA Press, 1470 Irving St, NW, Washington, DC 20010.

Journals

Letters to the Churches, translation of Cartas a las Iglesias, published twice monthly by CRISPAZ, 701 S. Zarzamora, San Antonio, Texas.

Challenge, published three times yearly by EPICA, 1470 Irving St, NW, Washington, DC 20010.

Central America Report, published six times yearly by the Religious Task Force on Central America, 1747 Connecticut Ave, NW, Washington, DC 20009.

Basta, published three times yearly by the Chicago Religious Task Force on Central America, 59 E. Van Buren #1440, Chicago, Ill. 60605.

Solidarity and Support Organizations

The Ecumenical Program for Central America and the Caribbean (EPICA) provides workshops to grass-roots organizations in the United States on Central America, and through its program for democratic institutions in El Salvador it supports the University of El Salvador. Address: 1470 Irving St, NW, Washington, DC 20010.

SHARE-NEST Foundation supports local initiative projects in El Salvador and arranges for delegation visits of sister parishes and communities. Mailing address: Box 16 Cardinal Station, Washington, DC 20064.

Semilla de Libertad Foundation, United States-based support group for the Christian Base Communities of El Salvador, arranges delegations to El Salvador, speakers and fund raising for Base Communities of El Salvador. Address: 529 S. Wabash Ave, Chicago, Ill. 60605.

Voices on the Border arranges visits to the repatriated communities in Morazan, speakers and financial support for these communities. Through the VIDA Fund it raises support and provides access to credit for sustainable development in El Salvador. Mailing address: Box 53081, Washington, DC 20009.

Campaign for Community Development Alternatives (COCO) facilitates direct community to community relationships to support sustainable development in El Salvador, particularly in the provinces of San Salvador, Cuscatlan. and Cabañas. Address: 609 East 29th St. Indianapolis, Ind. 46205.

National Debate for Peace in El Salvador, lobbying group for the broadest consensus-building group in El Salvador. Address: 110 Maryland Ave, NE, Washington, DC.